THIS ABOVE ALL

HOW TO LIVE AN ARTISTIC LIFE

JASON CANNON

IBiS
BOOKS

THIS ABOVE ALL: HOW TO LIVE AN ARTISTIC LIFE

Published by Ibis Books, 2349 Hyde Park Street, Sarasota, FL, 34239.

First edition

ISBN-13: 978-1-956672-02-2 (Paperback edition)

ISBN-13: 978-1-956672-03-9 (Ebook edition)

Praise for *This Above All*

"Jason Cannon's book is a must-read. Especially if you are an artist, want to be reminded why you become an artist in the first place - or just have always wondered if you could lead a more artistic life. Its honest and transparent and yet deeply witty and insightful look into this entire profession made me want to get back out there and do it even better. Easily the most truthful and yet inspiring book out there on the making of theatre."
—*Sean Daniels, Artistic Director, Arizona Theatre Company*

"There are some doozies in *This Above All: How to Live an Artistic Life*, that straight-up revolutionized my thinking. It is a guidebook to both theater and life that needs to live on every creative person's nightstand. I highly recommend."
—*Sarah Bierstock, playwright of* Honor Killing *and* Grace's Land 2.0, *and Artistic Director, Pass the Salt Productions*

"The subtitle of Jason Cannon's *This Above All* is *How to Live an Artistic Life*. Cannon focuses on artists (especially directors, actors, and writers) in the world of theater, but his penetrating insights apply to anyone in any profession. The book is a series of short chapters filled with exhilarating ideas about how to live artistically, which is to say how to live passionately, how to live, as Cannon puts it, "with all your heart." You will be tempted to read the book through at top speed because Cannon's quick, exuberant prose pulls you along. But then go back to read slowly, to pause on the many epiphanies about living and learning and refusing to be false to oneself or to anyone (the keen analysis of the speech in *Hamlet* by Polonius, from which Cannon takes his book's title, is worth the price of admission). Reflect on each gem for an hour or two—and then keep on reflecting for the rest of your life."

—*Jeffrey Couchman, author of* The Night of the Hunter: A Biography of a Film

"This Above All is brimming with philosophical insights and practical advice for young artists starting out in the world. Cannon shares the wisdom gained from many years of artistic practice, providing the reader with powerful reflections on art, life, and truth-telling. Essential reading for anyone wanting to harness their passion into a meaningful and sustainable creative practice."

—*Deborah Brevoort, playwright of* The Women of Lockerbie *and* My Lord, What a Night

"Those who are struggling to make it in their chosen profession, are questioning what's missing, and haven't found their artistic mojo yet, will reap great benefit from reading *This Above All*. Jason's passion for living an artistic life struck a nerve the first day we met. *This Above All* reminded me that the world of business I live in can be much more meaningful and stressless when you slow down, take a beat, enjoy the scenery, and re-examine your purpose."

—*Joel Ehrenpreis, CEO, Business Therapeutics*

For all who would be brave.

STORIES TAKE FLIGHT AT IBIS BOOKS

The IBIS is sacred to Thoth, the Egyptian god of learning, inventor of writing, and scribe to the gods.

They are gregarious birds that live, travel, and breed in flocks.

And they are legendary for their courage.

ibis-books.com

FOREWORD

How do you live an artistic life when you're not an artist? Well, at least when you think you're not an artist?

In this book, when Jason talks about the importance of rituals and totems, he'll tell you briefly about a retired Green Beret who came to him for guidance on how to write his heart-breaking, redemptive story.

That was me. A Green Beret. Not an artist.

What he kindly omitted was that I was also terrified, heart-broken, and clueless.

I served in the Army for almost 23 years. Most of that time was spent as a Special Forces Officer. I spent a lot of my adult life in combat or getting ready to go back to it. That was my life: operating in low-trust, high-risk areas with elite forces. I loved it. I was at the top of my game, but it came at a cost.

I lost a lot of friends to war, and the after-effects of war. After leaving the military, I struggled to make sense of the loss, the guilt, and the sudden departure of my own purpose as a resident in the civilian world.

It wasn't pretty. I was no longer at the top of my game. In fact, I was at the very edge of checking out. Suicidal ideation and depression were becoming my new Battle Buddies in this dark part of my journey.

The only thing that kept me holding on was a story I felt was burning inside me. I didn't know what the story was, but I swear to God, I felt as if I would die if I didn't tell it. More importantly, I felt that, if I did tell it, it could heal me and maybe others. It could help bring meaning to this corrosive affair known as combat that was only talked about in B.S. Hollywood movies.

I didn't even know the questions to ask to get the answers I needed when I washed up in Jason Cannon's storytelling class. It was a communal, theater-style class, and everyone was friendly, but I was terrified. I felt so out of place and ridiculous, but I had driven an hour and a half to get to this damn class, and I wasn't going home empty-handed. So, after the class was over, I gathered my courage and waited patiently for the other students to dissipate. I approached Jason and told him I had been working on a play and I had no idea what to do next. "I'll help you, man," he said with his cheerful smile.

Over the next nine months, I signed up for every class Jason taught. I did private sessions with him on writing and acting. I read and watched every play he suggested. We huddled over my script with stubby pencils and stale coffee. We did lip trills, warmups, and physicality work. Over time, Jason gifted me the craft of writing and the craft of acting. Mind you, I had zero training in either. It didn't matter to him. He didn't care that I wasn't a playwright. He didn't care that I'd never acted. What he cared about was that I had something to say. I knew that he saw me, and I wasn't quite so terrified.

He saw I was willing to do whatever it took to get this story out of my gut and into the world. He didn't give me a pass because I was a war-weary veteran. It was quite the opposite: he pushed me hard. And, for the first time since taking off that Green Beret, I started to come alive. I was doing the authentic work that Jason talks about in this book. I could finally share this story and complete my own journey home.

On November 10, 2018, one day before Veterans Day, in a dressing room in a Tampa Bay Marriott, I wiped the vomit from my chin, pushed up from the porcelain bowl, and resumed the warmups that Jason taught me. A few minutes later, my play, *Last Out: Elegy of a Green Beret*, with me playing the lead, debuted in front of over 300 people.

At the time of this writing, the play has traveled to 16 cities with nearly 100 performances. It's a finalist in five arts festivals and has been performed for over 75 Gold Star Families. It has led to approximately 250 post-traumatic stress interventions, and has recently been adapted as a film that's streaming on Amazon Prime, VUDU, Apple TV, and Google TV.

But that's not what I am the proudest of from this piece. I'm most proud because it's no longer mine. It belongs to people who need it more than me. Holly, a Gold Star Mom, says that every time she watches the scene where my character "Danny Patton" talks to his son from the other side, she feels that *her* Danny is talking to her from the other side.

Jason showed me that anger, which my original script was dripping with, "...is nothing but lazy, self-serving, cherry-picking, proof-texting bullshit." He helped me tell the story from another place, a place of love. He showed me that "love transforms the energy of your anger into something constructive." That constructive force is peace for Holly, peace for countless veterans, and peace for me.

Jason Cannon made that possible for me. And, in this book, he makes it possible for you as well.

Art is food for the soul, and we're all artists if we choose to be. It's accessible to every one of us if (and this is a big IF) we are willing to let go of the ego, do the work, and, when the time comes, give it away to whomever needs it the most.

This book gives you the process and the road map to do this every day for the rest of your life. And in these crazy, troubled times, where materialism and mass technology mask the beautiful journey to the truth, that's really good news.

As we prepare to take *Last Out* to the next level, tension and resistance creep in stronger than ever. The imposter syndrome re-emerges. When I ask myself, *Who the hell am I to do this?*, Jason's words ring in my ears: "Control what you can. Release what you can't. Prepare, and prepare, and prepare, so that when it's your turn, you can pounce."

Let's do this! I'll see you at rehearsal.

De Oppresso Liber...

Scott Mann

PART ONE

TRUTH AND LIES

We all know that art is not truth.
Art is a lie that makes us realize truth,
at least the truth that is given us to understand.
—*Pablo Picasso*

Acting is all about honesty.
If you can fake that, you've got it made.
—*George Burns*

THE ARTISTS'S INVOCATION

I arrive at rehearsal for the play I'm directing. Usually this is in a studio space, except during tech week as the show hurtles toward opening. Then I'd head to the theater itself. But let's say we're in Week Two of rehearsal. So the studio it is.

I'm early, but stage management is already there, as they always are. And most of the actors, too, are already present, stretching with earbuds in, walking their track, checking their props, or warming up their voices with a cacophony of tongue twisters, lip raspberries, and lung-expanding elocution exercises.

Backpacks, water bottles, and snap-topped containers of snacks mark off little zones for each actor's home base. Once or twice a week someone takes it upon themself to leave a platter of baked goodies on the counter outside the rehearsal room door next to the coffee machine burbling non-stop to keep up with demand.

Quick tip. You ever need to get rid of leftovers, leave 'em on the counter outside a rehearsal room door. Theatre people are notorious scavengers. Do not get between an actor and free food. You have been warned.

Stage management has my "director's table" set up abutting their own. Theirs is covered in the tools of their trade: laptop, sound board, highlighters, pencils, erasers, calling script, prop lists, scene change spreadsheets, first aid kit, Kleenex, hand sanitizer, paperwork paperwork paperwork, all the ligaments and gristle that bind a production together.

My table is clear except for my copy of the daily call provided by stage management. I put down my backpack and lunchbox, pull out my script, my notebook, a pen or two, and one of the many worry stones I always carry, most gifted from my beloved partner, which I will rub and rub and rub between thumb and fingers, both to bleed off the extra energy that spills out once we get cranking and to prevent me from chewing on my cuticles.

I make sure my phone is silent, take a swig from my water bottle (I'll get a cup of coffee at first break). I check in with stage management: how are they doing, do they need anything from me, any surprises from production or updates on that costume piece we asked about? They ask where in the script I want to pick up. I tell them. They start setting up the furniture and props.

I walk the space, and the world of the play reemerges. The colorful stripes of spike tape on the floor stretch upward into invisible walls, stairs, and doors. I gently check in with each actor, careful not to disturb their process, but also letting each of them know they are seen. A handshake here, a fist bump there, maybe one of them has a quick question.

I get back to my table. I stand and I breathe and I watch and I wait for stage management to call everyone to order. They make announcements, ask if anyone has any housing issues or other concerns. They hand it off to me. Each stage manager comes up with a different nickname for me, depending on their personality and the vibe of the room. "Now listen to *el director*." Or "Take it away, *jefe*." Or "All yours, *Cannonman*."

I don't give orders. That's not what good directors do. Instead, I ask how everyone's night and/or morning was. I maybe share a funny little something or other that happened to me since we broke last night. I give space for anyone to share a 3am mind-strike of insight about our show or their character or that sticky scene we didn't quite crack yesterday.

And then... I speak the only invocation that ever results in magic happening, in creativity being unleashed, in the Muse being invited, in Art being forged, in Truth possibly being glimpsed...

"OK then. Let's get to work."

WHAT'S YOUR STORY?

I work in the theatre. I make three-dimensional, flesh and blood stories. I have done so for thirty years, twenty-five of them as a grinding professional. But what I'm about to share in this book is not intended only for my fellow theatre-makers. Don't get me wrong, if you make theatre, you'll get a lot out of these pages (at least, I certainly hope you do!), but choirs get plenty of preaching to. It's those of you who do not make theatre—and who may not make anything you might consider "artistic"—YOU are the ones I also hope to reach. Show biz or business biz, everyone pull up a seat.

Because something compelled you to crack open this book. Perhaps you feel stuck or held back from what you want to do or who you know you can be. Maybe you've developed the pesky habit of starting but not finishing. Chances are you're struggling to maintain passion and balance in your work, exercise routine, or relationships. And the notion of living an "artistic life" made you go "hrrrmmmm..."

So why do I think my experience making theatre can benefit you, even if the mere thought of getting on a stage makes your stomach heave?

Here's the thing about theatre: *it reveals what it means to be human*. This revelation happens not only for the audience during the couple hours they watch a piece of theatre, but also for the practitioners as they spend the thousands of hours necessary to create it.

And the practitioners are many, because theatre is hardcore collaborative. Theatre requires multiple artists and artisans plying their crafts simultaneously. The playwright builds the script. The director and various designers (costumes, scenic, lights, props, sound, projections, hair and makeup) build the world of the play. The drapers and stitchers, technical director and carpenters, painters and welders, electricians and board ops, props masters and computer programmers take all those designs—all that theory—and put 'em into practice, building clothes and walls and furniture, hanging and focusing lighting instruments, composing music and sound effects, scouring online stores and thrift shops for the perfect tea set or baseball glove (nothing screams "false!" more loudly than a prop that doesn't belong), and then the director guides everyone through the exquisite, agonizing process of polishing every scene transition and cue call.

All of that work is in service of the audience. Don't want empty seats, so spinning in the background you've also got the managers and marketers and payroll and volunteer coordinators, and over there buried in cables and spare monitors is the IT department making sure the website stays up and the box office can process all the tickets.

And all of *that* is in motion long before the actors show up for rehearsals. After all, an actor without costumes, lights, or advertising is just a naked person trespassing in an empty, dark room. Yikes.

But when it all comes together, you get those couple hours of an audience watching actors play pretend on the stage. All the revelations from the process of creation coalesce into the cathartic revelation of the event itself: *here, look, that is you on stage, and together we are all understanding a little bit better what it means to be human*. Theatre is collaborative. Theatre is empathetic. Theatre is communal. And this above all: theatre is *story* come to visceral life.

That is why I can offer this book to you, whatever your theatrical experience or lack thereof. There are so many entry points into the process, and you already instinctively understand the power of story. We all do.

Just last year, archeologists discovered a cave painting in Indonesia of a wild pig—ochre on stone—and dated it to about 45,500 years ago. *45,500 years ago*. That is pre-everything in terms of our modern cultural identities and national boundaries. You know what's really cool about this pig? It's part of a narrative scene. Not just a replication, but a *story*.

Humans need story. We always have. To shape it and to share it. We need beginnings, middles, endings. We need chapters, scenes, acts, intermissions. Such demarcations enable us to process the gob-smacking vastness of time.

Events barely exist. They are momentary blips, flashes of excitement or fear or joy. They run at us full tilt from the feared-or-yearned-for future, sprint through the blurry present, and lunge through the tape into the receding past, where they stay for good, resting and rusting.

This is something I tell actors in rehearsal all the time: if your character is telling a past-tense story, it's only and always for a present-tense reason. Focus on the reason, and the story will tell itself.

Don't come at me with "memory." Humans have notoriously poor memories. Memory is curated, self-serving, and malleable. Our perceptions are limited and our points of view subjective. Our biases and presuppositions filter every stimulus before we even know what our senses are telling us. We are none of us as rational and insightful as we'd like to think. So we craft narrative, because memories and impressions only make sense as story. By retelling an event, we polish it, exercise it, preserve it as a story.

Story is not WHAT we remember; it's HOW we remember at all.

And it matters very much what stories you tell, listen to, write, and perform. The stories you ingest shape your view of the world. The stories you tell reveal everything about your intention toward the world.

Telling stories is how we move from where we were....to where we are now... to where we're going. Telling stories is how we heal, how we validate, how we inform, how we connect, how we convince, and how we make sense of the senselessness of the world. Myth. Legend. Fable. Allegory. Parable.

Theatre sprang out of religious festivals. That is no accident. Nor is it an accident that to this day any religious service you attend oozes with theatricality—costumes, props, a stage, a congregated audience, the re-telling of stories.

Stories are delivery systems. Depending on the intent of the teller, stories can cure or poison. The words "gospel" and "gossip," after all, share an etymological root.

And get this. The order in which a chef serves courses in their restaurant... the ebb and flow of taste and texture, the precision of the plating and even the shapes of the dishes... is a story.

A business plan... is a story.

A sales pitch... is a story.

A lawyer's closing argument... is a story.

A sporting event or the ups and downs of a team's season... is a story.

A marketing campaign... is a story.

The arrangement of an endcap display in a grocery store... is a story.

Show biz or business biz, we are all of us, every day, whether or not aware of it, telling and listening to stories.

And theatre? Well. Theatre is storytelling on steroids.

EVERYTHING IN THE THEATRE IS A LIE

That set is not a living room. Not a battlefield. The walls are flimsy and meant only to last the run of the show before being repurposed, recycled, or thrown away. And you might have noticed the fourth one is missing.

That sublime color in the light? It's not a sunrise. And the birds chirping, heralding the dawn? A digital sound file triggered by a finger pressing a computer key. It's all a carefully calibrated combination of lighting instruments and speakers, gels and wires, designed to seduce the audience's senses just... so.

Manipulation, pure and simple.

Those props? Fake. That bourbon those progressively drunker characters are chugging? Watered-down iced tea or sugar-free apple juice.

Those jaw-dropping costume changes? Rigged. Underdressed. Designed to fool and thus delight you.

That actor? She's not a valkyrie, despite her sword. He's not a prince, despite his crown. They're not the citizens of a besieged city, despite their groans and torn garments.

And those lines the actors speak? Not spontaneous. Not suddenly occurring to them to say. Those lines are rehearsed and polished, timed and honed.

Everything in the theatre—and I do mean absolutely every-thing—is a lie.

Everyone knows it. Even the audience. They buy a ticket, walk through a lobby, sit in a completely artificial setting. They look at a playbill, see the actors' bios. They know everything they are about to witness is a lie.

The job of the actor is to lie to people who know they are being lied to... and convince them they are telling the truth.

And you know what? Despite all the lies—or rather, be-cause of them—a well-done piece of theatre will transform the shared experience of the audience into catharsis. And in the throes of that moment, Truth may decide to whisper from the wings or even grace us with a glimpse of Itself.

Or not. Such is the indifference of Truth.

But the audience and the actors, every time, come together to seek. We go through the rituals—picking up tickets at will call and putting on costumes in the dressing room, ordering drinks in the lobby and putting on make-up, reading playbills and hearing "places, please"—and agree to believe that when the lights go down... and we take a breath together... and the lights come up... the lies will fuse into story...

... and the story will be True.

EVERYTHING IN THIS BOOK IS TRUE

Unlike the theatre, nothing in this book is a lie. Some of it will be theory, much of it will be practice. We need both. Because theory without practice gets us nowhere, while practice without theory gets us lost. Push-pull, yin-yang, they bloody each other's noses and keep each other honest.

So. All my upcoming ruminations on art and ego and discipline, on balance and focus and courage. All my offerings on how to mine your creativity and live an artistic life, even if you've never considered yourself an artist. All my stories and fun facts. It's all true. That does not mean it's all Truth.

A fact is true. It is not Truth. And it cannot control what you do with it.

Take a bunch of facts, like bricks, and stack them together. Build something. A wall, an edifice, a road. Those structures are a reflection of Truth. But they are not Truth.

My road might lead somewhere yours does not. Or they might reach the same destination but by different routes. I might build a cottage while you build a castle. My wall may keep storm waves at bay while yours protects our flocks from predators. Our roads may diverge, our walls may be different heights, your castle may lord over a hill while my cottage nestles in a valley, but you know what we'll be able to talk about for hours?

The fine art of working with brick.

The most effective ways to mix mortar. Our preferred trowels, plumb lines, and patterns. We may even compare the callouses on our hands. We'll walk our roads together and be able to pick out miniscule details that a few days ago our eyes would have skimmed over. I'll compliment you on laying your bricks in such a way that your castle can withstand attack while you'll whistle in admiration of how I laid the bricks in my cottage to maximize heat retention in winter and heat release in summer. You'll be grateful my wall keeps your field from flooding, while I'll give thanks that my sheep and cattle are safe. And our next creations working within the medium of brick will be even more delightful and effective.

The work itself is far closer to Truth than any fact. And I don't mean "work" as in the final product. I mean WORK as in the act of building. The action. The activity. The sweat equity. The art.

The artist—whether composing a symphony, building a bridge, or writing a report—focuses on the act itself. On the process. The artist knows the outcome will take care of itself if only they focus on the work.

As the artist works, layers of scales fall from their eyes, so they see a bit more clearly... a bit more clearly... a bit more clearly...

Because ultimately art is not a thing at all.

It is seeing.

ART IS SEEING

The cast and I were doing some fine-tuning music rehearsal on the big final encore song of *Buddy: The Buddy Holly Story.* I and my musical director Spiff—an incredible fellow who can play over a dozen instruments at the professional level (and even several simultaneously!)—had been very intentional about creating a room where "best idea wins." The cast was comprised of several ridiculously talented musician-singer-actors, and while I had taken piano lessons for a year as a kid and dabbled in choir in college and can karaoke a mean Sinatra and had somehow early in my acting career finagled my way into getting hired into the choruses of a few musicals, I was under no illusions. This cast would have a lot more musical insights than I, and Spiff and I insisted they share them.

So, as is the case with big final encore songs, there were several 16-bar sections built in for the various instrumentalists to take a spotlight solo moment. Shred a guitar. Slap a bass. Rock some keys. Wail a harmonica. We came up on a section that, as written, was intended for Buddy Holly. We noodled it for a couple minutes and then the actor playing Buddy, another mind-blowingly talented fellow named Michael, stopped and said, "Hey, I just had a solo last song, and Seth back there on drums hasn't had one yet. Can we give this one to him?"

First of all, just consider that for a moment. This is the lead. The STAR. This is the dude playing Buddy friggin' Holly in a show called *The Buddy Holly Story*. For him to have that level of big picture awareness, to be so in tune with the needs of the show, to be so willing to release his ego in service of the work? That is artistry in motion.

Spiff and I glanced at each other and grinned. *Best idea wins*. I turned back to Michael and said, "But of course. Seth, take it away."

And THEN... holy expletive on a stick. I got to watch a platinum-level drummer create from scratch a jaw-dropping drum solo. For ten minutes, everyone ceded control of the room and the music to Seth. He experimented. He conducted. He asked for the guitars and bass to back off, to come in a beat later, a beat earlier. He asked the keys to punctuate his snare, no no wait, the hi-hat. Horns, blast on two. Everyone wait for the pickup. Fiddle fiddle paradiddle. By the end of those ten minutes, Seth was sweating. The entire room had pulled into trench-deep focus. They ran it once more from the top. Seth smiled and gave me a thumbs-up. We all awoke as though from a shared dream.

And dreaming isn't that far off. Because for most of those ten minutes, Seth's eyes were closed. He was seeing something we couldn't and working to bring us into the know. He actually was seeing something that didn't even yet exist. He was, as they say, *in the zone*. Much like you'll hear athletes at the highest level talk about the game slowing down.

My mother is a professional soprano, gospel galore. I grew up watching her bring congregations to tears. She also often closes her eyes as she accesses the Truth in the songs she shares. When she closes her eyes, she is seeing ever so clearly, and the notes she sings are infused with the emotions she feels as she sees that which is beyond sight.

So, when I say "art is seeing," I am not devaluing the other senses or prioritizing literal sight. I am speaking of the proverbial "mind's eye." All of our senses, in their ways, are able to see. To perceive. To understand. To have "sight."

Lemme hit you with some Greek, because Greece is the well-spring of the theatre of Western traditions. Our word "theatre" comes from the Greek *theatron*, which translates as "viewing place" or "a place of seeing." Fun fact: *theatron* actually refers to the area of the amphitheater where the audience sat, not to be confused with the *orchestra* ("dancing space") where the actors performed or the *skene* ("tent") that was the precursor to modern scenery and sets. *Theatron*, like "church," can also mean the people themselves. Both the seats and the seated.

Do you see? The whole point of theatre—of any art, I would argue—is that the *audience* sees. It's not enough merely for the *artist* to see. When the artist sees something, in the way only they can, they then do their art in order that others may see it, too. Seth's drum solo. My mother's song of faith. Hopefully, this book. Expressing one's self is a means to the end. And that end is creating relationship with the audience—whether viewer, listener, or reader—so that they may come into a deeper understanding of their humanity.

Living an artistic life means you keep on looking till you see. Because art is not a *what*. It's a *how*.

ART IS ESSENTIAL

During the pandemic lockdown, a poll was taken and the general population listed "artist" as the least essential job in our society.

Essential.

I have to wonder how many of those polled only maintained their sanity through quarantine because they listened to music. Read a book. Watched a movie. Consumed art.

Or the flip side. Clinging to meaning in an unmoored world. Playing or composing music. Writing poems or plays or novels. Filming epic movies in the backyard. Hell, baking bread. Yeast, like toilet paper, was often in short supply, remember?

Essential. Boy oh boy, we figured out fast which workers out there were truly "essential," didn't we? My buddy Kyle worked at Trader Joe's through the worst of it. You think there isn't an art to deescalating irate grocery shoppers?

Here's the thing. Art is food for the soul.

Do you remember every single meal from last month? Of course not. Well, maybe if you're journaling or food planning, but you'd still have to double-check your records. Never mind, here's the point. Do you need to eat every day? Absolutely. Even if you can't recall what you ate, you know you did. The same with art. So while food helps our bodies grow and fuels our daily activities, art helps our minds and hearts and humanity grow, fuels our daily evolution.

Art makes it easier to breathe. Art may not be how we stay alive, but it's why we live at all.

This is why art is *essential*. It provides context, it carves meaning, it gives us a framework to make sense of our lives and a world that so often seems senseless. And as we learn to create art, we learn to see the inherent creativity and artistry in those around us.

Art happens... all the time... all around you. You don't have to be in a theater. Or a concert hall. Or a museum. You can be in a supermarket. Or an office. Or a factory. Or a farm.

You just gotta let yourself see.

ART IS NOT PRECIOUS

Though it is essential, art is not precious. Art does not reside in an ivory tower, surrounded by a moat, with a heavy iron gate that opens only if you know the secret password. It is not esoteric. It does not belong to the enlightened few.

Art is not a riddle to be figured out. Art does not require pinched brows and knowing, nodding "hmmmms."

Chaucer. Big-time literary heavyweight, right? Well, if you haven't yet, check out *The Summoner's Tale*. One of the most epic fart jokes in all of storytelling history. Not merely a fart directly into a friar's face, but then a serious discussion of how to divvy that fart up into twelve equal parts, so as to share it with others. Scout's honor, that joke lives in (ahem ahem ahem) pinky-sticking-out *literature*. It's awesome.

Shakespeare. Needs no introduction. Get this. Shakespeare was *popular*. The Netflix of his time. Hot romance. Kick-ass fight scenes. You ever seen *Hamlet* done well? That dude is hilarious. Tragic, sure, that's in the title, but he's also the wittiest guy in the room. Keep digging into the Bard, Stratford's own Billy Wigglestick. Cross-dressing. Mistaken identities.

Twin siblings causing *Parent Trap*-esque plot machinations. Clowns. Music. Songs. Magic. Like *literal* magic. Hell, one guy even has his noggin turned into a donkey head and the "ass" jokes come so fast you can't keep count.

Shakespeare wrote for everyone. Elevated and insightful in one scene, ribald and bawdy in the next. Not because some of us are elevated and others of us are bawdy, but because all of us are *both*.

It's vital to entertain. In fact, entertainment comes first. Entertainment is not a dirty word. Art must entertain and delight the senses, or no one will pay attention. Art is not about "message" or "theme." Those are by-products. If the audience ain't paying attention, your "message" ain't gettin' through. Spoonful of sugar, baby. And it doesn't matter if your spoon is silver-plated or carved from wood.

Art belongs to all.

Just remember this. Shakespeare wrote in iambic pentameter. That's a fancy poetry term for a line of verse that rhythmically goes like this: *duh DUM duh DUM duh DUM duh DUM duh DUM*.

You know what else goes like that?

duh DUM duh DUM duh DUM duh DUM duh DUM.

Your heart.

ART IS ASSERTIVE

Living an artistic life means living assertively. Ever confident yet ever humbled by the work.

Art is not aggressive. Art is not full of itself, does not force itself on others with false bravado. It doesn't get in anyone's face, using volume and false outrage to pull focus. "The lady doth protest too much." If it comes from a place of integrity and merciless editing, then art never needs to explain itself.

Nor is art passive. Art does not play coy or play the victim, does not sit in the corner passing silent judgment. Art does not offer false apology. Art does not hide.

Art does not set out to preach, convert, or convince. Art attempts to understand. Only after vigorously seeking to understand does art then dare seek to be understood.

Art is not interested in win-lose, all-or-nothing, zero-sum games. Living assertively means seeking outcomes that are win-win. It means holding your own space and boundaries while simultaneously recognizing that others are entitled to hold theirs. I teach my young actors to always try a note twice. Sometimes in rehearsal the director will give a note that you do not agree with, that you absolutely know will not work. But maybe the director is seeing something you can't. Win-win. Try the note twice. Twice because the first time you won't be able to give it a fully honest attempt, you'll still be working through your own resistance to the idea.

The second attempt will yield one of three results. Either the director will say, "Nope. I was wrong. Go back to what you were doing." Or you will say, "Whoa. That actually works. Awesome." Or you both will say, "Hey! That just opened up something over here behind door number 3! Let's try that now!"

And in every case, the play has been improved, because even if you just go back to what you were already doing, you'll see it with fresh eyes.

ART IS VIOLENT

Art is violence. Theatre is violence. Remove the pejorative baggage. It's like a doctor: do no harm, but this may hurt.

Here's the thing. Creation requires violence. Creation literally alters the state of matter. It changes something from *this* into *that*. And there's nothing humans hate more than change. So think of violence as the effort and energy required to effect change. The pickle jar goes from stuck to open only through grunting and straining, hitting it on the counter, running it under water, using a towel, maybe resorting to using one of those plastic grippy things, and once you torque it hard enough... POP. Violence. Even more—you bite that dang pickle. CRUNCH. Violence. Transforming brined cucumber into bodily fuel.

Likewise, art is violent. Theatre is violent. Break it down with me. SPEAKING is violent. You have silence... and you speak into it. You destroy that silence, transform it. You have a vowel sound. *Ee ay ai oh ooh.* That vowel sound can continue indefinitely until you introduce a consonant. Consonants are cleavers, chopping vowels into words. You can't hold a 'd' sound. It bites off the vowel. Violence forges meaning. Violence is transformative.

Painting is violent. Writing is violent. You have a blank canvas, an empty page, and then... paint splatters. The keys strike a letter, a word, a sentence onto the page. You have fundamentally altered that canvas, that page.

Music? Violent. You *pound* the keyboard, yes? You *blow* through any wind or brass instrument. You *pluck* strings, or *strum* them, or *fret* them, all active verbs that imply energy upon them, stress upon them, violence upon them. Hell, when you do a sculpture, you literally hit the rock with a hammer and chisel.

CHOOSING is violent. It costs. And when you recognize that cost, paying it becomes your choice. You claim your agency by paying for it. The classic marriage vow... forsaking all others? The act of courage is saying no to everyone else, so you can say yes to the one. Same thing in rehearsal. Choosing THIS gesture means saying no to every other gesture you tried.

Violence must be specific. Generality no one gets. You must get painfully, microscopically specific, and only in that specificity will you find universal Truth. Specificity is why we can keep performing Shakespeare, because otherwise why bother? It's been done. But not done THIS way in THIS time by THIS company for THIS audience with THIS director and THIS cast and THIS design team in THIS venue within THIS current social/political/economic environment. Every time you specify a THIS... you are doing violence.

Violence is the energetic cost of your creation.

ART IS RELEASING EGO

True story. I was trying to convince a theatre, any theatre, to let me direct John Patrick Shanley's gorgeous play *Doubt*.

Out of the blue, my friend and colleague Kim called. She was starting a new theatre company. First production? *Doubt*. And did I want to... play the character of "Father Flynn"?

Argh!

"Kim, I've actually been aching to direct it."

"But Jason, you'd be perfect. I'm playing 'Sister Aloysius.' I need a killer co-star. And you're who I want on stage with me."

"But Kim—first, wow, thank you—seriously, I know I could crush it as director."

"So do both."

Flabbergasted silence.

That level of trust? Dare I?

Inspired by Kim's daring, I dared.

I worked my ass off. I analyzed every syllable of that script. I asked three of the best directors I knew to come in at various points in the rehearsal process and note the hell out of me.

The generosity of that community of artists took my breath away.

If you've read it or seen it (and if you haven't, you oughta), then you know there's a big "did he-didn't he" mystery hanging over the whole thing. As the actor, it was important to know where my Father Flynn lived, what he had done, what he believed, where his torment sat.

I had heard that John Patrick Shanley—Tony Award-winning John Patrick Shanley—was actually a pretty cool guy. Accessible. Put his contact info in his playbill bios. I had also heard that he and Philip Seymour Hoffman were often seen whispering in the corner during shooting of the film version.

OK. Dare I?

I dared. I spent a good hour typing up my analysis, my take on the story, my understanding of the character, and how I intended to approach the production. I couched it all in terms of "I don't want to mess up your play, kind sir, you don't have to tell me every little secret, but like just let me know if I'm wackadoodle off in left field somewhere."

I sent the email. Expecting nothing.

Five minutes later. DING. Pulsing in my inbox was an email reply from none other than Tony Award-winner and screenwriter of *Moonstruck* John Patrick Shanley. I imagined him strolling down 42nd thumbing away on his phone.

I eagerly opened the email. This is what it said. Word for word. In its entirety.

"Jason. Play whatever backstory you want. Have fun with it. John."

Flabbergasted silence.

My first reaction was a bit huffy, like "I just spent all this time writing this epic, in-depth, brilliantly analytical email, and that's all you're gonna give me?" (Aren't humans fascinating?

JASON CANNON

I expected nothing. Got something. Took umbrage. We are ridiculous creatures.)

But then, after a moment, I thought... WOW. What an absolutely gigantic gift Tony Award-winning John Patrick Shanley just gave me. He taught me something. It wasn't the generosity of him taking 20 seconds to email back some stranger half a continent away. It was the demonstration of his artistic soul and lack of ego.

See... *he gave away his play!* He gave it away to *me*. Without ever having met me. With no precondition.

What. The. Hell.

Here's what I learned: no one "owns" a play. Or any piece of art, really.

A playwright gives the play away to the director. The director gives the play away to the actors. And the actors give the play away to the audience.

Theatre, by its very nature, is an exercise in releasing ego, in giving away what is most precious and meaningful. True of any art form. Your painting hangs above someone else's sofa. Your book is tucked into other people's backpacks and you cannot control when or where they read it, whether they dog-ear the pages or use a bookmark (please use a bookmark!). Your music gets played by high school students with squeaky reeds and by virtuosos in concert halls.

You must give your art away. And you cannot judge what the audience thinks or feels about it. You must offer, with no precondition. You must sacrifice. And then the act of releasing your art will change not only the audience... it will change *you*.

Thank you, Mr. Shanley, wherever you are.

SERIOUSLY, ART IS RELEASING EGO

There's nothing quite like the feeling of powerlessness a director has on opening night. Everyone has something to do... except you. All these people you've been sweating and grappling with the last few weeks in rehearsal, they go to work that night, while you... sit and watch. Or pace the lobby trying to hide your armpit sweat. Nothing to do except second-guess every damn one of the tens of thousands of decisions you made on the production over the past many months.

That feeling begins at a very specific moment. It's the split-second after the final rehearsal ends. In regional theatre, this is typically the Friday afternoon a few hours prior to opening, after we've worked through any last notes and fixes from the previous night's final preview. There comes a moment when I thank the cast, and wish them all "break a leg tonight," and the stage manager says "OK, we're broken, your call tonight is 7:30." Rehearsal ends. And in that moment, the director goes from having the most power in the room...

snap... to having none. You go from being the person everyone is asking for everything... to the person from whom no one needs anything.

Your work is finished. The actors and stage manager and crew still have jobs. They switch from creation to replication, but still. They have work. They've got art to do. And you, the director? Cut loose. A vestigial tail.

(I must thank my colleague Kate Alexander for sharing with me the following metaphor, because it brings me such comfort in my work. I offer it to you; adapt it to your particular profession as you wish.)

People think the director is the captain of the ship. This is not so. The stage manager is the captain of the ship. The cast is about to set sail and have adventures the director will know about only if they read the show reports, like messages in bottles washing ashore. If a mast snaps or a sail tears, the cast and crew will have to handle it on their own, and the director can only trust they built a vessel strong enough to withstand the storms.

Because that's what the director is. The ship builder. The director knows every square inch of that show, has walked every board, tested every pulley, double-checked that the bilges pump and the larder is full.

But when the gangplank pulls in, the director is left on the pier, watching the ship work its way through the harbor, out into open sea, and as the curtain closes on opening night, the ship disappears over the horizon.

The ship builder goes to sleep. Wakes the next day. Heads to the docks.

And begins to build another ship.

EDGING GOD OUT

A young actor once shared with me that her grandmother taught her that *ego* stands for "Edging God Out." I liked that. Edging God Out. Whatever "god" means to you.

But don't you have to have an ego if you're an actor? Or any artist? Aren't you saying, "Hey look at me! Look at my work!"

For every famous artist you know, there are thousands, tens of thousands, grinding away in anonymity, going daily to the smithy of their souls to forge something meaningful with their creativity.

At the end of the day, the mission of the actor, of any artist, is simply to move the body of work forward. Ninety-nine-point-nine-nine-nine percent of the world will never know my name. Never see me perform, never see a play I directed, never take my classes, and—unlike you, oh wise Reader—never read my books.

The number of Shakespeares in the world? The ones who can change the world from the top down? That number is infinitesimally small... and they don't do that on their own. We are all interconnected. There are as many molecules of air in one breath of air as there are breaths of air in the entire atmosphere. There are as many molecules of water in one glass of water as there are glasses of water in all the Earth's oceans.

Shakespeare doesn't happen without every other actor and playwright plying their craft before him, and doesn't come to be "Shakespeare" without every actor and playwright toiling away after him. That old chestnut "bloom where you're planted"? Well, the field is only a field if each individual blooms. The random Shakespeare-tree that grows out of that field? Its very tree-ness is only apparent because of the field surrounding it. The tree owes itself to the field.

So... does my work not matter? If I only ever am part of the field?

It's up to you to believe that what you do has meaning. No award, no review, no press or prestige or fame or riches untold will ever convince you of your value if you don't already believe it. True in show biz. True in business biz.

If you and your work aren't enough without it, you'll never be enough with it.

TRUTH AND THE LEAF

All this talk of theatre and art. So what? What does it all serve?

Imagine a tree. Your favorite kind, so long as it has many beautiful leaves. Now imagine an ornery breeze blowing through them. See the leaves fluttering and dancing.

Hold that image in your mind. And understand that each one of those fluttering leaves is a *feeling*. Each one dancing, each one calling attention to itself.

And now understand that every single one of us contains a canopy within.

Now imagine someone pointing to a single leaf and proclaiming, "There! That is The Truth." Even more, imagine that someone plucking that single leaf from the tree, snapping it off at the stem, then holding it up—limp, the life force draining out, the color already rotting around the edges—and proclaiming, "This leaf, and only this leaf, is The Truth!"

Nonsense. Willful ignorance. Manipulative tomfoolery. Abject bullshit.

Such is the way of the charlatan. The way of many of our politicians and preachers and gurus and would-be teachers.

"Ignore the rest of the tree," they say. "This is the only leaf that matters. The only leaf that is True."

Let's say you point to the branches and ask, "But, hey, y'know, what about all those other leaves?" Rare is leaf-plucker who will reconsider their choices and thank you for the reminder. More likely they will fly into a rage and spittle-shriek at you: "ONLY THIS LEAF ONLY THIS LEAF!" Your audacity to question them may even drive them to cut down the entire tree. That would be a loss, yes. But such an act does not wound Truth. The wind will find other leaves in other trees, and the charlatan will be left without shade.

Yet we fall for it. Again and again. Because it's *easy*. You cannot hold an entire tree in your arms, but you can hold a single leaf in your hand. You can possess it. Get lost in its individual veins and wax poetic about the conspiracies within. You can abdicate responsibility and be done with the daily work of learning and growing. You can quiet the buzzing, insatiable voice of curiosity with the smug, heavy breathing of absolutism.

You can press it in a book, try to preserve it. But it's dead.

No matter what you do, it will never dance again.

TRUTH AND THE WIND

What if we consider the entire canopy? Crunch the numbers, write a gorgeous algorithm to account for every leaf, even factor in the branches, trunk, bark, and roots... surely that is Truth?

If only.

Here's the thing. The leaves do not move of their own accord. Feelings are not the cause, they are an effect. The wind that animates them... we see the wind's impact but not the wind itself. That is what the best of us work to understand. Our prophets and professors and preachers, our scientists and historians and journalists, our gurus and coaches and mentors and teachers. Those who do the hard, daily work of stripping ego and agenda out of the equation and who attempt to grasp the wind.

All cultures give names to the various winds based on directions and severity, what you might call the winds' personalities. Winds blow through every pantheon. So then. Surely the wind is Truth?

Actually, no.

For what is wind but air molecules in motion? Wind is not its own cause. There is a force that sets those air molecules a-tumbling before they bump into our leaf-feelings.

There's a wonderful linguistic treat in the Greek word *pneuma*. Modern pneumatic tools used compressed air. That's because *pneuma*, depending on context, can variously mean wind, air, breath...

... or *spirit*.

So. This force that animates the wind? Call it whatever you like. The Muse. God. The Universe. I call it Truth, or at least the closest approximation to Truth I can currently discern.

There are moments... and I do mean mere moments... when the best and humblest among us stumble into moments of transcendence. And in that transcendence, they receive a message from the life force that deigns to energize—or not—those air molecules, transforming them into wind.

These moments are not gifted willy-nilly. One can only ever work to create the circumstances in which such moments may manifest. You cannot force them. They have nothing to do with luck. You are not somehow more special than someone else if you receive such a moment and they do not, or vice versa.

You may have noted above, in my list of practitioners and professionals who are working to grasp Truth, that I did not mention the actors, directors, dancers, musicians, or singers; the painters, poets, composers, or writers; the sculptors, architects, or designers.

The artists.

I did not leave the artists out. I couldn't even if I wanted to. Because the artists—the ones who work with integrity, day by day—*are already there*.

Grasping the wind is what it means to live an artistic life.

And that is why, even if your profession is not in the arts, you can still live and work artistically. Inviting artistry into your work elevates your work into an offering. Seeing the world through an artist's eyes empowers you to identify (and thus avoid or ignore) the charlatans. Freeing your inner artist allows you to feel the cooling breath of Truth on your brow far more often.

TRUTH IS INDIFFERENT

Unlike us humans, Truth possesses no ego. Why should it? It has nothing to prove.

Truth doesn't need your praise, your support, or even your defense.

Truth is not insecure. We are.

Truth simply IS. It has been here long before you, me, or anyone working through their insecurity by attacking it. It will be here long after you, me, and all our bickering have faded.

When someone attacks Truth, they cannot hurt Truth. Swords can't cut it. Spears can't pierce it. Fists can't strike it. The wind simply swirls around the slice, stab, or punch and moves on.

You'll recall the falsest among us, the charlatans, pluck a single leaf and claim the Truth has been given only to them. Truth is exclusive, they say, and available to you, sure, but only from them, and only if you believe a certain way or think a certain thought or open up your wallet and send in three easy payments. Oh, and don't you dare deviate or they shall cast you out and revoke your membership and cut up your cool-kid card. Such actions do not harm Truth in the slightest, but do devastating damage to the charlatans and those who have chosen to follow them.

Many saviors and gurus and teachers have said, "The Truth will set you free." (I also enjoy the addendum "but first it will piss you off!") They are one hundred percent correct. But not because Truth cares about setting you free. Truth doesn't seek us out, hoping and intending to free us. Why should it? It has nothing to prove. It has no ego.

When we glimpse Truth, we are set free simply because that is what Truth does. That is its function and its purpose. Truth is incapable of *not* setting us free. It actually has no choice in the matter. We are lucky that is the case.

The wind blows indifferently on all, yes? It's up to us to turn our faces into the breeze, to hoist the sail, to raise the flag, to fly the kite.

Truth's indifference is powerful stuff. It'll keep you humble, if you let it.

TRUTH IS NOT A FEELING

We cannot "earn" Truth. We can only work, day by day, to create those circumstances under which Truth may grace us. And even then we'll only be able to go, "Oh. Oh! OH! Did you see that? Did you *see*?" Like a meteor streaking, or a lightning bolt crackling, or a dolphin leaping, or a green flash winking as the sun sets at the beach.

And when we try to capture it, write it down, tell someone else about it, it's like describing a dream that was so incredibly vivid but no words you string together come even close to doing it justice. It's not the Truth that is limited. It is us. To take some liberty with G. K. Chesterton, we can totally put our heads into the heavens, but if we try to put the heavens into our heads, our heads'll split.

Because, ultimately, humans are not *above* the natural world. We are *part* of the natural world. We may have evolved (which we didn't earn), but that doesn't make us special.

We are feeling creatures who think, not thinking creatures who feel. We strive to be reasonable and rational, but look around. Heck, look at yourself. We are an unreasonable, irrational species. We are masters of self-justification. And it's not about logic. The wackjobbiest conspiracy theorist employs exquisite logic. Their logic is impeccable. Logic can easily be reverse-engineered to "prove" any whopper of a presupposition.

"But it feels *right."*

So what? A feeling is one damn leaf. That's different from intuition, which is someone taking in an entire canopy and going... "Oh. Oh! OH!"

The artistic life requires rigorous self-examination and the constant interrogation of our feelings. Because our feelings don't "mean" anything. They have no agency or intent. They simply are.

Your feelings are not lies. But neither are they unto themselves Truth. Your feelings can be in conflict with themselves. That's OK. Everyone, no matter their profession or position, feels that conflict and confusion. You don't have to justify that conflict with self-serving logic. Let your tree have many leaves.

An artist doesn't justify. When someone lives an artistic life, focused on the work and cranking hot as a professional, there is no need to justify. Because the output will be true.

TRUTH IS THE SUN

One last metaphorical crack at defining "Truth" for the purposes of this book.

Truth is the sun.

You cannot look directly at the sun for more than a moment or two. We know it's True not because we see *it*, but because *by* it we see everything else. Much like we don't see the wind, but we see its impact.

But here's the thing. Seeing Truth is not a static situation. Nothing about how we perceive Truth is stationary, and we have to be cool with that. That's the *work*.

As the day passes, the angle of the sun's light creeps through degrees. Thus the light's hue oozes through the color spectrum minute by minute. We see differently at dusk than at dawn.

That ever-changing angle also affects the shape and length of shadows. Hidden things become visible. That's awesome. But the reverse is also true. Visible things become hidden, so when our sight is compromised, we have to rely on measurements and tools and know-how. On artistry. The sailor navigating... what if clouds roll in? Are you still pointed in the right direction? Will you be willing to course-correct when the clouds part and you catch another glimpse?

Even the very Earth upon which we stand is in constant motion, hurtling through space at 1.6 million miles per day (over 18 miles per *second*), and spinning on its axis. Except even that spin is variable, depending on your latitude. If you bundle up and trudge to either pole while I strip down to my skivvies and stand on the equator, in one day I'll spin 24 thousand miles while you in that same day simply spin in place. One revolution each, but wildly different mileage. Which is True?

If you and I are time zones apart, we will see the sun differently at the same time. And it must follow, as the night the day, there will be times we see the sun *not at all.* Or see it as waxing and waning moon reflections.

The tilt of our Earth's axis also means that the light of Truth bounces on us differently in winter than in summer. Set your alarm for sunrise and you'll awake at different times throughout the year. The sun does not change. We do.

If we are gazing at our tree, the pattern of light is ever-shifting, not because the Truth is shifting, but because our situation, our circumstances, our perceptions are shifting. And do not forget, in addition to all the cosmic spinning and hurtling, the very fluttering of our leaves also affects how the light bounces. It's not that Truth is a moving target. The Truth simply is. But my oh my, the work we must put in to perceive it. The patience. The humility. The willingness to compare what I see with what you see with what they see.

And ultimately, this is the benefit of living an artistic life. By grasping the wind and seeking Truth, your world expands. Your empathy grows. Your capacity for grace increases. Your stress and anger reduce, because you no longer assume the worst of those who see differently. Truth reminds you of big pictures. Truth helps you finish strong. Truth keeps you present and aware. Truth and the process of art encourage you to aspire while grounding you in reality.

Truth is not an easy fix. Truth is not a short-cut.

Truth is the sun.

SO WHAT?

My first college holiday break, I headed home with my mind blown, sure I had been lied to my entire life.

I was taking a class called "World of the Bible." It was taught by the brilliant Dr. Thompson, who had also—fun fact!—been professor to my parents. This class focused on the physical evidence of biblical history. The dust and rock. The rivers and commerce. What people wore and ate, how they travelled and communicated. It was Theology stretched upon the rack of History, and Archeology was the menacing, masked muscle cranking the gears till tendons popped.

My childhood faith was being hardcore tested. As it should be for everyone, frankly. But oooooh I was frothy. First chance, I cornered my dad and went on my rant. It had something to do with the brand new discovery (of course it was brand new only to me) that—*gasp*—translation between languages wasn't necessarily 100% accurate! In fact, translators fought all the time, and politics was involved, and the biases inherent in language could skew things, too. The horror!

"Dad! DAD! Did you know that Dead Sea Scrolls *this* and Septuagint *that* and Latin Vulgate *this* and the Hebrew for 'virgin' can also just mean 'young woman' as in 'with child' as in translation can be self-serving and how can something be a prophecy if there's a political agenda or circular logic? Huh? HUH??"

On and on I went, making perfect, outraged sense in my 18-year-old mind. My dad, bless him, sat quietly and nodded. If I ever make a movie of this moment, I'll have the actor playing my dad polish his glasses with a trying-not-to-show-it bemused grin.

I finished. Probably I was panting.

My dad put his glasses back on. Took a breath. Exhaled it through his nose. Looked me right in the eye and said...

"So what?"

I never asked, but my gut tells me perhaps he learned this pedagogical trick from Dr. Thompson.

Here's the thing. My dad did not mean it dismissively. I think back on that moment and it rings like a bell, pristine and clear. That moment irrevocably altered my understanding of how to think. At least, that's how story has shaped my memory of this moment.

I do not recall the rest of our conversation. But I do remember we wrestled, sometimes with each other, sometimes side by side with an idea big enough to take us both on at once. "So what" didn't end our process. It BEGAN our process. It continues to this day. "So what" is the fundamental question of the artistic life. It keeps you humble. It keeps you open. It propels you forward.

"So what" means... have your feeling. Let it flutter. But then forge ahead: *so what?* The initial feeling is never the whole Truth.

Translation can be political. OK. So what? Does it then follow that we should just throw up our hands and give up? Baby with the bath water? Or... what might political tension reveal about the largesse of your God? Is prophecy about the future, or about the present? A bit of both? Juicy juicy.

A word can bulge with multiple definitions. OK. So what? Does it then follow that nothing means anything? Or... why did Translator A choose *this* while Translator B chose *that*? Might you find an intersection? Might their disagreement open up an even truer path? Yummy yummy.

"So what" reminds us that *definitive* does not mean *absolute*. Definitive is a temporary status. Marlon Brando's take on "Stanley Kowalski" in *A Streetcar Named Desire* is definitive for his time: *"Steeeellaaaaa!"* But if it were absolute, there'd be no reason to do the play again.

We often speak of artists (and thinkers, and tech innovators) as being "ahead of their time." Cool, right? Shakespeare was *ahead of his time*. But just how far ahead, hmm? How long does "definitive" last? And which specific aspects of the work are "definitive"? Any average fourth grader today knows far more about science and technology and basic health and hygiene than Shakespeare ever did. Just because he was ahead of *his* time, does that mean he is forever and always ahead of *all* times? No. We must be discerning. Like panning for gold. The glimmering pieces of Truth revealed in his work... see, that's the stuff that's *timeless*.

Our work is never absolute, even though it can be definitive. The body of work moves forward, sometimes because of us, often despite us. We learn more. Uncover more. Evolve more. And so Truth continually finds new ways to manifest Itself to us. Or not. Such is the indifference of Truth.

Example from my rehearsal room. When directing musicals that incorporate popular songs—I've done everything from

Burt Bacharach to Chuck Berry to Buddy Holly—my musical director and I work closely with the actors to find what we call the "emotional tempo" of each song. Here's what that means: go listen to the original "Great Balls of Fire" by Jerry Lee Lewis. Or the original "That's All Right" by Elvis Presley. To our modern ear, they sound positively pedestrian! Sloooow. Way way way too slow. Were they always that *slow*? Technically speaking, yes. Their tempo is their tempo. But think how that tempo must have *felt* to the newly forged teenagers hearing that music for the first time. That tempo, when first heard almost 70 years ago, was earth-shaking. Incendiary. So damn *fast* that parents clutched their pearls.

So what happened? Did the music change? No. But the body of work moved forward. Our communal understanding of tempo adjusted as musical tastes, technologies, and abilities evolved. Those musicians who were ahead of their time? Well, time caught up. It always does.

In rehearsal, we therefore have to tap into the Truth of those songs, which means increasing the tempos, sometimes significantly. Other times, we find we have to slow a song down, make it gooier and sexier, especially the "making out in the back seat" ballads. Replication would be far easier. Because not only are we trying to capture how the songs originally *felt*, but we are also building a *live performance*. The audience isn't listening to a recording or snapping on headphones. They aren't paying to experience the music intimately and individually. They are paying to feel the music viscerally and collectively, all up and down their body and soaking their skin. They don't want the music poured discreetly into their ear; they want the music gushing all over them, splashing and oozing and dripping. They want to be swept up in an auditory tidal wave that may even wash them into the aisles to dance unabashedly with their neighbor.

Emotional tempo. Truer for that particular production than the tempo of the original (definitive?) recording. And if I ever direct any of those shows again, I'll have to forge, in collaboration with the new musical director and cast, the truest emotional tempo for that production at that theatre with that audience. I'll have to redefine definitive, yet again. And the only thing I know going in is that if I try to be ahead of my time, I'll produce crap. Others can decide what time I belong to. All I've got is the present, and if I care more about my legacy than about giving that audience the jolt they need to dance in the aisles, my work will be false. And nothing stinks like false crap. True in show biz. True in business biz.

More examples of how "definitive" is delightfully subjective. Check it out...

Go into any sports bar. Stand on a table and ask everyone really, really loudly whether they'd rather start a basketball team with Magic Johnson or Larry Bird, Michael Jordan or Kobe Bryant, LeBron James or Stephen Curry. Find yourself a booth and watch the fireworks. Even more. What if that sports bar is in LA? Boston? Chicago? Cleveland? San Francisco? You better be ready to duck and cover.

Nadal, Federer, or Djokovic?

Just how many "Director's Cuts" of *Bladerunner* do we really need? (At last count, there are eight different versions out there...)

Did you know Edward Albee went back and re-edited *Who's Afraid of Virginia Woolf?* Because times and language and audiences had changed. That play won every award in the universe and has been taught for decades. You can't even get the rights to perform the original, "definitive" version anymore.

I just read that the new *Top Gun* sequel, *Maverick*, assembled its final cut out of 800 hours of film. *800 hours*.

49

That's over 33 days of film. Which two hours—out of a MONTH—are definitive? Boy howdy is that an interpretive pickle.

What's your family's most treasured recipe, the one you'd never give out to anyone? What if you and I are cooking at different altitudes? What if one of us needs gluten or dairy free and has to make substitutions, or the market was out of that particular brand of vanilla that day? What if your grandmother invented that dish living somewhere with thicker humidity than where I'm trying to replicate it? What if my oven has a hot spot? What if the pan itself affects the cook, like with my grandma's fruit cocktail cake, and that pan is no longer manufactured?

Definitive?

How many takes of a song in a studio? Which studio musicians are on call that day? How about unplugged? Where are the master tapes? Wanna remix 'em? Wait a year or two, someone will drop a cover. Maybe they'll outsell you, just like Patsy Cline's "Crazy" is now far more "definitive" than Willie Nelson's, even though Willie wrote the darn thing.

Even good ol' ahead-of-his-time Shakespeare. Paper was expensive. The printing press was way too costly for theatre-makers back then. Actors were only given handwritten copies of their own lines. Shakespeare died before any of his plays were published; he didn't get final edit. YEARS after he died, actors in bars pulled together scraps of cue scripts and snippets of their own memory to rebuild his plays. Even then, it was editors who added those act breaks and stage directions. We've got quartos competing with folios, and to this day Shakespeare-lovers battle tooth and nail over whether Hamlet says "sullied flesh" or "solid flesh." (Sidenote: it's "solid." Come at me.)

So, yes. A word that means both "virgin" and "young woman" has problematic gender politics baked in. And yes, a translator may feel pressure, internal and external, to make sure the New/Second Testament story fulfills the Old/First Testament prophecy.

But so what? Don't dismiss or disengage. Interrogate. Excavate the emotional tempo. Let the talking heads perform their desperate, manufactured, self-serving debate about what's definitive and who's ahead of their time; they have nothing to do with your work or your art.

You know what has everything to do with your work and your art? It's simple, if not necessarily easy. It's not a secret formula or a magical spell.

It's practice.

PART TWO

PRACTICE MAKES PRACTICE

The knowledge that every day there is something more to learn,
something higher to reach for, something new to make for
others, makes each day infinitely precious. And I am grateful.
—*Uta Hagen*

You've got to learn your instrument.
Then, you practice, practice, practice.
And then, when you finally get up there on the bandstand,
forget all that and just wail.
—*Charlie Parker*

ART REQUIRES PRACTICE

If the Muse-wind blows by, and you are not practicing, it will not linger to fill your sails.

When I say *practicing*, I mean it every way. I mean acquiring proficiency in your thing. I mean maintaining proficiency in your thing. I mean mastering your thing. And I mean the carrying out of your thing. Doing the actual work. Heck, if you're a doctor, you have a medical *practice*. Attorney? Law *practice*.

A mile is always a mile. The time in which you run a mile may change, but the mile does not. How the mile feels to you as you run it may change, but the mile does not. When you practice, it doesn't get easier. You just get better. Practice forges talent into skill, and skill into expertise.

Sounds like practice makes perfect, right? Occasionally, that is true. But far more often, the truth is this. Practice... makes practice.

I confess to stealing this idea from my beloved partner, who is a wonderful yogi and skillful yoga teacher. I apply it to

JASON CANNON

theatre, to improvisation, to writing, to cooking, to running, to loving her day by day.

Practice makes practice.

In yoga, your body is your body. No more, no less. And each day, your body is what your body is. Not the same as yesterday, different from tomorrow. So while you may get into your flow, do a sun salutation and breathe into your poses, you must grapple with this fact: your body will never again be exactly what it is right now. Comparison is the thief of joy, and joy is right damn now.

Likewise, do not compare yourself to the yogi on the mat beside you. Different heights. Longer or shorter legs. Bigger or smaller feet. Thicker or thinner torso. Your pyramid pose, side plank, and triangle will differ from your neighbor's. But you can both be right.

Poses are not absolute. They are guides.

This means your tree pose, humble warrior, or crow will only ever be "perfect" for the splittiest of split seconds. And even when you nail it, as you continue to breathe, you'll find yourself going deeper. And deeper. Just when you think it can't get any more balanced or exquisite, you'll exhale and discover another quarter inch of flexibility, another ounce of strength.

Tomorrow? That same pose may prove elusive. Or you'll have gone for a run and have a tight hammy and have to avoid that pose altogether and focus on something else.

Progress, not perfection. Perfect—like definitive—is only ever a temporary state, and usually catches you by surprise. So if your practice does make perfect, take that moment to feel your joy and say your huzzah. Then continue your practice. Because there's no end point. It's a process.

Practice makes practice.

PRACTICE REQUIRES PREPARATION

Preparation is a process. You may be tired of me calling everything a process. But it's true.

Living an artistic life is a daily choice. This means you must prepare—and re-prepare—every day. It's not something you do once and have it on permanent lock. Simple, not easy.

Each day is its own step of the journey. So each morning you must not only flip your sign to open, you must also each evening close up shop. If you leave your paints uncovered overnight, they dry out. If you don't wash out your brushes, they become brittle. Your quills and pencils need resharpening. Your pen will run out of ink. Using a tablet to write? Better recharge it.

Pianos fall out of tune if not maintained. Same with guitar strings: watch any musician, they constantly re-tune. And sometimes those strings break. When I'm directing musicals, we always have back-up guitars—re-tuned every night—sitting offstage for when the actor's instrument needs a sub. One of my favorite cast gifts I ever received was after I directed a production of the musical *Once*. The cast saved all their broken strings and wound them into a large mason jar, creating a piece of art that sits on my desk.

Preparation is a process. You must invest in it.

You wake. Your muscles are tight. Your mind needs to spin up. Your bladder is full. Your mouth is dry. You are in no state to go to work. Preparation is getting ready for work. Preparedness lives just down the block from discipline. Discipline is the art of being prepared.

Prepared doesn't mean you know what's going to happen. Prepared means you anticipate possibilities and probabilities while leaving space for improvisation and inspiration. Your backpack can't carry every tool you might need for every potential eventuality. Weigh yourself down too much and you won't be able to hike, much less climb.

Prepared means you're willing to do the best you can with what you've got. Take what you need, leave the rest. Understand that mostly what you need is you.

Remember, there is no way to know when the wind will blow. The Muse, God, the Universe, Truth... they go where they please, when they please. When they turn their eye on you... you better be working. And if they deign to visit, you better be prepared to host.

In practical terms, this means preparation requires routine, ritual, and invocation. Keep your work space organized and welcoming. Keep your tools in accessible places. Build a routine (which is simply a repeating pattern), even just a couple minutes' worth. You don't have to plan this pattern entirely in advance; you can excavate it from the small, daily things you already do. Add a sprinkle of intention. Boom. Routine.

My alarm each morning is the grinder in the coffee machine kicking on. I give my beloved partner a kiss on her head or arm. I scratch Dog One behind the ears; he's usually burrowed under the covers. I sit up and step into my slippers, shrug into my robe. Already my body understands what is happening, even if my mind hasn't caught up. I pass by Dog Two and pat her on the head; she has moved out to the couch at some point in the night. I get a coffee mug. I turn on a light and leave it low for when my beloved partner gets up in the next hour or so. I drink a mug of water. I take a probiotic for my gut health with a second mug of water. I leave the mug by the coffee machine. I walk into my office. I boot things up and stretch a little. I give myself the time it takes for the coffee to finish brewing to scroll some news headlines, check the score of yesterday's St. Louis Cardinals game, review and add to my list of tasks in my bullet journal. My synapses are firing less in fits and starts and more in patterns. My senses tingle. I smell the coffee before the machine chirps. I head back, fill the mug steaming full. Back to my desk.

Now for totems. We live in the relative, tangible world. Embrace the power of totems. Objects of power that lift routine up into ritual. You can think of them as souvenirs from your far-flung adventures. Their power is subjective, but no less vital for being so. My jar of broken guitar strings means nothing to anyone else but means an entire world to me. To you it's cute. To me it's memory and feeling and encouragement and proof my work matters.

I set my mug down on a coaster that was a gift from a student; it's stone and has a Gaelic infinity symbol. As I sit, I look at my desk. It is covered in totems. A piece of driftwood and a large shell, both of which I pulled from the Pacific while visiting the Oregon coast with my beloved partner. A prosperity stone that was a parting gift from a former colleague. A small engraved wooden box with treasures inside: a miniature Gandalf that my aunt gave me when I was a kid, a perfectly spherical worry stone that my beloved partner gave me early in our relationship, a stopper from a bottle of exquisite bourbon that I drank with a close friend during vacation, and two poker chips. One is an oversized, metal, commemorative chip from a retired Green Beret who came to me for guidance on how to write his heartbreaking, redemptive story, and the other is a clay Vegas chip gifted to me by an actor friend during a late-night game, not long before he passed away from a heart attack at the goddamn age of fifty.

All of these totems throb with unseen power and whisper to me as I sit. I glance at the walls and shelves surrounding me. Pictures. Pieces of art. Souvenirs and gifts. Vision board. Finisher medals from 10K's and half-marathons. Baseballs—one an errant foul ball that almost clobbered me as I was standing in a concessions line, the other the very ball I threw out as a first pitch at old Busch Stadium.

And my whiteboard. The last thing I look at before I hit my first keystroke of the day. The white board has my word goals. Royalty payout schedule. And reminders. A reminder to back-up my work every day. A reminder of the working title of my current primary project. Other random notes that needed capturing. And this reminder, which is my daily invocation: *Write Bravely, Edit Mercilessly*. The purpose of the invocation is to keep you humble, to prevent your ritual from becoming precious and prescriptive. The invocation welcomes those powers larger than yourself to visit that day, should they choose to.

Then I start typing. Some mornings I have awoken with a chapter practically splitting my head apart, and it's all I can do to get it out. Other mornings the cursor sits there, taunting me, blinking and blinking and blinking and blinking. Most mornings, the words come in spurts for the first twenty-ish minutes. And then I find a groove—or rather, the groove finds me—and I crank for about an hour. Is it good? No idea. I'll figure that out later.

My beloved partner is up. We have our morning routines and rituals together. Exercise and dog walk and breakfast and conversation and plans for the evening. She goes to her work. And I go back to mine. I haven't churned out all my words yet.

There is genius in routine, and ritual is simply a code that unlocks you. Your combination differs from mine. Your combination will evolve as needed: my little Gandalf is almost four decades old, but my whiteboard has only been around a few months. I tell my acting students all the time to adjust their physical and vocal warm-ups—their preparation ritual—to the demands of the show. If you're gonna swing a broadsword, you've gotta prep differently than if you're singing a solo than if you're doing a softshoe than if you're speaking vast tracts of verse.

Control what you can. Release what you can't. Prepare and prepare and prepare, so that when it's your turn... you can pounce.

PRACTICE REQUIRES DISCIPLINE

The performance was going gangbusters. Full house. Cast locked in. And the big Act Five broadsword battle between me as "Hotspur" and my good buddy Matt as "Prince Hal" in our rollicking production of *Henry IV, Part 1* was sizzling. Sure, Matt was destined to win and give the big speech over my dead body, but I got to deliver the death speech! Oooooh my goodness, how actors LOVE to deliver the death speech. You need some scenery chewed? Just tell an actor they get to die on stage.

Anyhow, our fight choreographer had set us up beautifully. I got in a few licks, but then the tables turned. Matt wounded me, gashed me good, and the whirling cyclone of attacks and parries came to a sudden stop as I stood downstage. I looked out over the audience—into the life beyond—and flexed my molars, crunching the blood capsule tucked in my cheek. (Sidenote: it is no easy feat to keep a blood capsule tucked in your cheek while grunting, screaming, and swinging a broadsword.) I coughed, both to show the audience how wounded I was and also to manipulate the red-dyed corn syrup coating my tongue, and blood oozed down my chin. Bad ass.

Then, the climactic finale. I took a heaving breath, loosed one more bloodthirsty yawp, turned and charged at Matt with my sword held high above my head. One last, desperate, two-handed chop to snatch victory. But Matt was ready. He stepped forward, ducked low, and sliced his sword across my gut as my slash cut nothing but air. I crashed into the steps, crumpled and broken, but still aware enough to turn my face up into the beautiful light cue for my death speech.

It had gone that way every night, every show. No real blood, no actual cuts, maybe a slight bump here or there, as any athlete deals with. But on this night... I let the electricity of that audience get to me. My discipline wavered, and my adrenaline spilled out of its channel, flooding and befuddling my senses. As I sprang around for my final attack, mouth perfectly bloody, I charged too hard. I lost control. Matt, bless him, executed his move perfectly, but when I crashed into the stairs, I cracked a knee on the floor, smacked a forearm on the corner of a step, and whacked my temple but good on the corner of another step.

Hotspur took a little longer to roll over that night, and his death speech probably didn't make much sense. He also had a slight limp the next performance, and the bruise on his arm, though hidden by costume armor, definitely put a hitch in the giddy-up of his broadsword swinging the next couple days.

Here's the thing about stage combat: the audience must never fear for the actor, only for the character. Otherwise, they are taken out of the story. Maintaining the illusion requires unimpeachable discipline. And not just for that one audience at that one performance. If I had concussed myself, or broken my forearm, or shattered my kneecap, I wouldn't have been on stage for the next audience at the next performance.

Even though the show went on, Matt and I had to adjust the fight. It wasn't quite as bad ass. My lack of discipline dented the integrity of the production.

Discipline and integrity are next-door neighbors.

To live an artistic life, you must have discipline. But—you see this coming, right?—discipline for the artist is not a noun. It is a verb. Discipline is not a thing you have. It is a thing you do. DOING discipline can be as straight-forward as consistency of replication, unlike my Hotspurred example above. Discipline is DOING what needs to be done, when it needs to be done, even (and especially) when you don't want to do it.

Discipline is simply remembering what you really want, because if you focus on what you want—and I mean truly focus, no "wouldn't it be nice" or "if I only had the time" multitasking bullshit—then you will instinctively prioritize, and all the distractions will fall away. Or at least have a lesser vote in your daily assessment of what it is you want to achieve.

Discipline is choosing between what you want *now* and what you want *most*.

Discipline is dying safely, even when the show is crackling, so you can give your awesome death speech every performance from opening to closing.

PRACTICE REQUIRES FOCUS

You may have heard of the 10,000 hours theory, supported by research and discussed by Malcolm Gladwell and even rap-referenced by Macklemore.

Here's the thing. The amount of practice and rehearsal you put in matters. Sure. But the *quality* of that practice and rehearsal is even more vital.

If you half-ass your practice, your performance will have a butt-cheek missing. Good luck finding pants.

So how do you ensure your practice is of sufficient quality? One word. FOCUS.

Without focus, your practice is just killing time (and you cannot kill time without injuring eternity, as the man in the woods said). We have made a fetish out of being "busy." Our "busy-ness" is ego. It makes us feel important. But really, "I'm so busy" is an excuse, a way to avoid Truth. In silence we'd hear the breeze, maybe even hear ourself, so we let the noise in. When training for longer races, especially half-marathons and longer, it is important to focus on quality miles rather than what we runners call "junk miles." Burning through shoe tread simply for the sake of saying you piled up the mileage. So what?

My god do we love to be distracted.

Humans are not evolutionarily hard-wired to be multi-taskers. Multitasking is nonsense. Picasso said that art is simply the elimination of the unnecessary. So get rid of distractions. Set an intention. Ask yourself what the purpose of any rehearsal or training run or work session is and stay on target. Leave your mother-bleeping phone *off*. Use your breaks to actually reset your mind and re-harness your creative energy. Breaks are crucial.

Focus.

Likewise, you've gotta rest. Focus earns you the space to rest, because focus enables you to make more progress in less time. Without rest, without space, without stillness, you will burn out. Your junk miles will wear you down and leave you unable to race when it matters.

Athletes know this. Where do you think the home-field/home-court advantage comes from? Check the research. As much as we would like it to be, it's not us fans screaming in the stands. It's REST. Not having to travel. Not having your Circadian rhythms kneecapped by time zones.

Soldiers know this. They sleep every chance they get. Rest is a weapon. Take away the enemy's rest, they will be compromised.

Parents know this. What is the sweetest gift a new parent can receive? Six straight hours sleep.

Chefs know this. When that gorgeous, sizzling protein comes off the grill, do they cut in right away? Hell no. They let it rest.

Composers know this. Sheet music is littered with rests. And those rests, even more than the notes, shape the music. Mozart: "The music is not in the notes, but in the silence between." Debussey: "Music is the space between the notes." Artur Schnabel: "The pauses between the notes—ah, that is where the art resides."

The artist knows that time spent walking, reading, lounging, meditating, hanging out with friends, *resting* is not time wasted. The field must lie fallow. The battery must recharge. The muscle must recover.

Focus.

Nothing drives a director batty faster than an actor who doesn't write down notes or blocking. Because giving the same note twice? Means I won't be hiring you twice. Write it down. I don't care if you're blessed with perfect, crystal-clear memory and recall. Don't forget you're in a collaborative environment. Show that director you take them and their input seriously. Write it down. I guarantee it'll help you remember it, too.

Focus.

Leave all the crap of life at the rehearsal room door. It'll still be there when rehearsal is over. Use rehearsal to escape, to play, to be present, to work, to be human.

Focus.

Consistency of replication is paramount. The 8pm performance on Wednesday has to be as entertaining and effective as the 3pm on Saturday as the 7:30pm on Sunday as the 10am on Tuesday. True not only in show biz, but also in business biz, yeah? So understand that focus and professionalism are roommates. It's actually not all that difficult to get something right. It is the enthusiast, the amateur, who practices something until they get it right. It is the professional who practices something until they can't get it WRONG.

Legendary cellist Pablo Casals was asked why he continued to practice at age 90: "Because I think I'm making progress."

A master is simply someone who has failed more often than any enthusiastic has even tried. Mastery is repetition multiplied by focus.

PRACTICE REQUIRES REPETITION

Repetition is the key to learning. Repetition is the key to learning. Repetition is the key to...?

Yeah, you got it.

Likewise...

The only way to expertise is repetition. The ONLY way to expertise is repetition. The only way to EXPERTISE is repetition. The only way to expertise is REPETITION.

As Bruce Lee said: "I do not fear the man who has practiced 10,000 kicks one time. I fear the man who has practiced one kick 10,000 times."

There may not be a lot of difference between your 1001st kick and your 1002nd kick, but there will be a world of difference between your 1002nd kick and your 7854th kick. This is the essence of expertise. Of mastery. Of rehearsal. Of effective replication of performance, whatever your biz.

At the same time, the only arbiter of "real artist" or "good artist" is YOU. But note this: being a good artist does not instantly mean all of your art is effective. Far from it. Being a good artist means not only can you tell the difference when this bit of your work smells like roses while that bit of your work smells like crap, but you also then have the strength and integrity to pitch the crap out.

Recognizing repetition as the pathway to expertise keeps you humble, keeps you working, keeps you focused outwardly: on the emotional response of the audience. Not their praise. Their emotional response. Do not seek their praise. Seek their catharsis. Their praise is fleeting. Their catharsis alters how they interact with the world.

Keep kickin'.

PRACTICE REQUIRES ACCUMULATION

Think of sporting events. We focus on moments of winning. The buzzer-beating jump shot. The ninth-inning walk-off home run. The overtime goal. But those moments resonate only because of all the tension and build-up. And I don't just mean on the court, field, or rink. I mean the quiet, precise preparations in the locker rooms. The taping up, tying up, stretching out. And even before that, the work, the practice, the sweat equity invested long before game night. That dedication is all part of the accumulation of meaning.

You can't force change or progress or transformation. You can only, day by day and bit by bit, work toward creating the circumstances in which they may happen. Think of it this way. Snow falls on a branch. The branch holds because the weight of each additional flake is negligible. But snow continues to fall, and the branch discovers it's groaning a little, and then there comes a point when one more flake is one too many, and the branch snaps. And we perceive the snapping of the branch as having been caused by that one last flake. But no. That flake had no more and no less to do with snapping the branch than any other flake that came before.

We have no control over the branch. On stage, the story has already been written, and the job of the actors is to tell the story clearly and passionately. They know the branch will snap, the audience knows it will snap, and the catharsis is in discovering together how it will snap. But in real life, we don't know and can't know when the branch will snap. We can only keep adding snowflakes.

How many steps in a marathon?

How many words in a novel?

How many notes in an opera?

How many heartbeats in a life?

How many kisses in true love?

Is any step or kiss or word or note or heartbeat more important than another? Objectively, no. But if you run a marathon, you know which step feels way different from all the others? The last one! The one when you cross the finish line. But it's the thousands of steps before that enable you to perceive that one step as special. Meaning is achieved through accumulation. This does not mean we have no agency. It means our agency is the size of a snowflake. It means our agency... shocker!... is a process.

Listen to this. I was directing two shows back to back, *A Clockwork Orange* and *Hamlet*. I was at auditions for *Clockwork*, but also had *Hamlet* in the back of mind, watching the actors for potential fits in either show. Two young men both gave very strong auditions, Jared and Luke. I knew I was going to cast them both, but wasn't sure who fit where. I finally decided to cast Jared in *Clockwork* and Luke in *Hamlet*.

At the first rehearsal of *Hamlet*, Luke met Jill, who was also in the cast. They hit it off, to put it mildly. Before opening night, they were an item. By closing, they were a couple. Fast forward a few years and they were married with kids. Can I "take credit" for that relationship or those kiddos? Not in any sense of having foreknowledge, but if I had reversed Jared and Luke, the fate of many souls would've been fundamentally altered.

And don't forget, since we're jamming on the idea of agency, the only reason Luke got cast is because he gave a great audition. And you know what he did in that audition that caught my attention? He did a damn *cartwheel*. He's the only actor I've ever seen do a cartwheel in an audition. That choice could've imploded as a gimmick, but he pulled it off. Luke's agency—"I'm gonna do a cartwheel!"—had repercussions far beyond his intention. If he doesn't do that cartwheel, does he get cast? Does he meet Jill? Do his kids come to be? Without that cartwheel... how might things have turned out?

Never know which snowflake may snap the branch.

Think of time travel. *Back to the Future. The Terminator. Avengers: Endgame. Star Trek 4: The Voyage Home*. All these movies, these time travel stories, they depend on us believing that tiny actions in our past can have huge ramifications in our present. The pebble in the water sending ripples to the shore. A cartwheel. Snowflakes.

Your present is your past for your future. If you believe that changing a small thing in your past could drastically impact your present, then why can't doing some small thing today, in your present, impact your future the same way? Best day to plant a tree? Twenty years ago. Second best day? Today.

You don't know what the outcome will be when you take that small action. Scattering seed. Some will take root. Some won't. But still you scatter. Because the only thing you know for sure is if you plant nothing, nothing will grow.

PRACTICE REQUIRES TIME

All that is required to write—poem, business plan, sales report, or symphony—is a pencil and some time. And that time must also include learning how to read and write, which is actually learning how to think.

The pencil is easy. The time is hard.

Composer John Alyward has noted that those who have not experienced making art always see the creative process as a luxury: "The big thing I got when growing up was, 'Oh, you're a pianist? I always wanted to play the piano. I never had the time.' I've always wanted to reply, 'Well neither did I.'"

Here's an easy equation. "Oh, you're an X? I always wanted to X. I never had the time."

That variable, X? Plug in whatever you're passionate about, whatever profession or biz you've chosen. Law. Cooking. Construction. Entrepreneurship. Anything that required you to invest your most precious resource... your time. Imagine someone saying to you *I never had the time*. That little shrug of a phrase? It diminishes your choice. But only if you let it.

"Well neither did I."

We've all got the same 24 hours in a day. How we choose to spend them...? Well. That's really the whole ballgame right there, isn't it?

PRACTICE REQUIRES MISTAKES

Several years ago, I was going through an incredibly difficult time. Lots of transitions. Lots of pain, most of it self-inflicted, and much of it inflicted from me upon others. Mistakes compounding and self-justification abounding.

I received a letter in the mail from my Aunt Vondria, my mother's youngest sister. She is a free spirit, an actor and painter and sculptor.

She had made me a little piece of art. A craft project really, just a few inches on each side, some pink-purple-coral construction paper, and somehow the colors were all woven together, intertwined like sea currents. I had no idea how she had created such a gorgeous pattern. On the back, this is what she wrote:

"This piece was made from an accident, a sad mistake. The entire pad of perfect construction paper got wet and the colors bled onto each other. After the paper had been discarded, it dried, leaving the pattern of the accidental spill in different colors on each sheet. I found it months later and thought it much improved. I love you. Have faith."

A picture of this flawed yet improved construction paper has been the background image on my phone ever since. I keep the original note and art on my corkboard at home. It is the most beautiful reminder I have ever received of a deep-seated truth of the human experience: mistakes, failure, pain... they are unavoidable, and to be cherished as the most teachable moments, as the opportunities for grace and discovery, as the tilling of our richest soil for our greatest art, insight, and maturation.

Samuel Beckett put it this way: "Ever tried. Ever failed. No matter. Try again. Fail again. Fail better."

Mistakes are not only unavoidable, they are necessary. As my Grandma Cannon loved to say, "If you don't have scrapes on your knees, you haven't had fun."

Living an artistic life means allowing yourself to make mistakes, and then figuring out which mistakes to keep. Mistakes are bricks in the road of practice.

Here's the thing. If you don't make mistakes, you're doing it wrong. Whatever your "it" is.

If you don't then learn from those mistakes—reset and do it again, only better this time—then you're really doing it wrong.

If you can't accept that you've even made mistakes, well geez. You're not doing it at all.

PRACTICE REQUIRES PAYMENT

Value is subjective. Something is worth what someone will pay.

Art costs you. Your time. Your energy. Your focus. Your intention. Your blood, sweat, and tears.

Is your art valuable enough *to you* to pay what it costs?

Obviously, I do not use the word *costs* merely in its financial sense. The true cost of something is the time you invest. Expertise costs time. Intimacy costs time. Traditions cost time, because a tradition only becomes tradition through repetition.

Preparation is investment. Practice is compound interest. Your art will be worth what you pay for it.

But here's the thing: your art is also worth money. How much? Depends. Something is worth what someone will pay. But do not apologize for expecting compensation. In the arts we tend to undervalue our work, or we are so eager for our work to be seen that we'll give it away at a discount or for "free publicity." My first "professional" acting gig? Three weeks of rehearsal, two-week run, only got paid if I helped strike the set after closing, and then I got handed my crisp twenty-dollar bill. You read that right. This company touted its shows as professional gigs. Twenty bucks. Break that down: time rehearsing, time working lines and prep outside rehearsal, time in tech, all the time in actual performance, tack on those two or three hours of strike... call it 18 cents an hour. And I was just so happy to have been on the stage and so grateful to have scored a credit for my resume that I took that cash with a grin and considered myself lucky. Dang. I shoulda framed it.

Step *Two* is convincing the audience your work is worth it. Step *One* is convincing yourself.

PRACTICE REQUIRES PASSION

Fun facts...

- Stevie Wonder was told by a teacher that he had three strikes against him—he was poor, black, and blind—so he should just forget music and make potholders.
- Walt Disney was told a mouse would never work.
- Oprah Winfrey was told she was "unfit for TV."
- Jerry Seinfeld was booed off-stage at his first stand-up performance.
- Fred Astaire was told he "can't act."
- Sidney Poitier was told to become a dishwasher.
- Steven Spielberg got rejected from film school three times, and finally finished his BA in 2002. For context... *Jaws* was released in 1975.
- Babe Ruth struck out twice as often as he hit a home run.
- Stephen King received 30 rejections for *Carrie*. And before those rejections started piling up, he had thrown the manuscript in the trash. His wife Tabitha dug it out of the garbage and insisted he finish it.

- Michael Jordan was cut from his high school basketball team. And even after he turned pro... well, he speaks for himself. "I've missed more than 9000 shots in my career. I've lost almost 300 games. 26 times I've been trusted to take the game-winning shot and missed. I've failed over and over and over again in my life. And that is why I succeed."

I could fill pages and pages with examples like these. My first professional audition was a travesty. I look back and wince. Everything I could do wrong, I did do wrong. But I also took huge lessons from that cringe-worthy audition. And that theatre company? Over the years, I ended up acting in two shows and directing three shows for them.

It's not that failures guarantee you success. It's that what you choose to learn from your failures empowers you to define what success even is.

Everyone mentioned above had something in common. Their practice was driven by voracious passion. But here's the thing about passion. It's not a feeling. It's... yes, you know what I'm gonna say... a process.

Passion is not euphoria or exuberance. Quite the opposite. The Latin root of passion is *pati,* which means *to suffer.* A passion is something you care about so deeply you are willing to suffer for it.

Understand that suffering is not the same as being tortured. Do not buy into the self-serving mythology of the "tortured artist." The point of torture is to break someone. The point of suffering is to redeem you, make you stronger, make you more able to identify the difference between those who work with integrity and the charlatan. The charlatan does not suffer. They are not willing to put in the work.

When you do strength training, you tear your muscle fibers. They strengthen by rebuilding themselves. Everything costs something.

Another word that shares that Latin root, *pati*? PATIENT. What a word. The noun is literally a person who is suffering and needs medical care. The adjective describes the capability to wait and to endure.

Passion... is *patience*. It is endurance. Running through that stitch in your side at mile 21 of a marathon. Shaking the lactic acid out of your fingers and playing your scales one more time. Refusing to lose the stare down with your blinking cursor when the words just... won't... come.

Lots of people say they feel passionate about something. The charlatan makes their living with such proclamations. Passion is easily faked. Do not be fooled. Passion is revealed only through gritted-teeth, enduring, daily, focused, insistent, even-when-you're-not-feeling-like-it, disciplined practice.

Period.

PART THREE

ACTING AND THE AUDIENCE

The actor is an athlete of the heart.
—Antonin Artaud

Your willingness to wrestle with your demons
will cause your angels to sing.
—August Wilson

WHAT IS ACTING?

Heads up. Part Three is going to be the most theatre-heavy and acting-centric portion of this book. But "all the world's a stage," yes? And "all the men and women merely Players." You, dear Reader—whether you are in show biz or business biz—you are already an actor. You've been acting for years, since you were wee and just learning about object permanence. Every day, you slide effortlessly between multiple characters: spouse and partner, friend and colleague, parent and child, sibling and rival, boss and employee, server and public. How many masks do you keep in your pocket, ready to slip on as other players enter or exit your scene, or as you move from one scene to another? Um, LOTS.

So keep that in mind as you consider what follows. You're already an actor, even if your stages are metaphorical. These lessons I'm about to spin from the literal stage... you don't need a secret decoder ring. Truth and Art belong to all.

But just to get us all on the same page, let's define our terms. What is acting? At its most fundamental, acting is simply behaving truthfully within imaginary circumstances.

Note that *truthfully* is a much larger word than *realistically*.

Also note that it's *behaving*, not *feeling*. It is, after all, called ACTING. To act. To do. We call 'em nominees for Outstanding Supporting Actor, not Outstanding Supporting Feeler. Don't get me wrong, feelings are vital, especially in the rehearsal process. But if your voice and your body don't translate your feelings into action? If the audience doesn't see it or hear it? They won't get it. True on stage. True in life.

Another great definition of acting is that it is simply standing on stage naked and slowly turning around. Metaphorically speaking, of course. Or not. (That's a story for later.)

An actor must simultaneously cultivate vulnerability and a thick skin. An actor must cede control while maintaining control. An actor must find themself in every character, and every character inside themself. They must exercise their empathy muscles to exhaustion.

If that sounds like a lot, just remember this: an actor must simply stand on stage—cloaked in every exquisite lie crafted by the playwright, director, and designers—and tell the truth.

But here's the thing about telling the truth. It's the hardest easy thing in the world.

WHAT DO YOU SEE?

The most important question I ask actors in rehearsal is this: "What do you see?"

The most important question actors can ask themselves during preparation and analysis, or when they are stuck in rehearsal and knocking their heads against a moment that won't budge, is this: "What do I see?"

The most important question you can ask yourself in life, when something doesn't make sense, when you're unsure which way to turn next, when Truth feels a million miles away, is this: "What do I see?"

Note that I'm not asking, "What do you feel?" Neither am I asking, "What do you think?" Nor am I asking that old theatre standby, "What do you want? What's your motivation?" All of those questions are important parts of the process, but none of them start the process. The catalyst for the process is always, "What do you see?"

When you are stuck, get the focus off yourself. Because it's almost never actually about you. *What do you see?* And whatever or whoever you see, what does it or they need? The target—the thing you see—will tell you what to do next.

I don't merely want to kiss my lover's hand. *I see a hand that needs to be kissed.*

I don't merely want to make a sale. *I see a customer who needs to be served.*

I don't merely want an apology. *I see a friend who needs to be forgiven.*

I don't merely want to win the game. *I see a trophy that needs to be hoisted.*

I don't merely want to save the day. *I see an innocent who needs to be saved.*

Do you see how *seeing* gets you out of your head? Asking *what do I see* reminds you that while wanting may fuel a scene, wanting never motors a scene. Wanting is invisible. But kissing, serving, forgiving, hoisting, and saving are playable verbs that manifest your internal life into externalized action, thus making it accessible to the audience.

When you actually see what you see (or actually hear what you hear, or actually smell, taste, or touch what you smell, taste, or touch), then you'll know what to feel, think, and want.

WORDS ARE BOATS ON THE SEA

In acting, words are boats on the sea. These vessels have import. They carry treasures in their holds and ferry sojourners from one continent to another. But it is the myopic actor who focuses solely on those boats without considering the depths they float upon. Before daring to speak, the actor has currents and trenches and coral reefs and schools of teeming life to behold and explore. If the actor ignores the sea, their boats may as well be lashed to poles in port with sails furled.

I am not denigrating words or the script. But a boat cannot travel on dry land.

Understand the playwright's job is not to create words but to trim them. To walk among the vineyard, cast a keen eye upon the grapes, and prune without mercy, so that the grapes remaining can access a fuller abundance of moisture and sun and become fuller and tastier. Therefore, the actor must treat the words with *more* reverence, not less. And that means taking into consideration the full context, the terroir (to stretch the vineyard metaphor to breaking!), the genesis of each word.

Remember also that the words in a play are spoken. They are dialogue. They do not exist for reading eyes but for listening ears, and so require mouths and muscles making sound. Back in Shakespeare's day, people didn't say to each other, "Hey, wanna go see a play?" They said, "Let's go hear a play."

Do not aim for "naturalism" with your speeches on stage. The situation is heightened. Even "realism" usually falls short. You are aiming for Truth. So take advantage of all the myriad facets of speech: pitch, rhythm, cadence, inflection, tone, volume, articulation, etc. Learn from singers how to infuse musicality into your speech. When you treat a word musically, you enlarge the emotional capacity of that word. Shakespeare's "O" is a great example. The vowel IS the feeling, and that feeling—that "O!"—can be rage, horror, desire, jealousy, joy, mourning, whatever the situation requires.

To accept words as the whole truth is to exist solely in the mental plane. But acting... theatre... art... life... is *visceral*.

The script is a map, not a recipe. A painting, not a formula.

POLONIUS ISN'T FUNNY

I took the title of this book from a little ditty called *Hamlet*. I'm about to break down the famous speech from which it comes, demonstrate the nitty-gritty of textual analysis and emotional interrogation, the grime-under-the-fingernails of doing art.

Act One, Scene Three. Let's set the scene. Polonius is bidding farewell to his eldest child, his son Laertes. Laertes is leaving Denmark for France. If you are unfamiliar with the play, just imagine a father sending his first-born off to college, you'll get the gist of the emotional context.

As Polonius is fussing over Laertes and Laertes is gathering up his carry-ons, Polonius offers a trove of fatherly advice:

> *Be thou familiar, but by no means vulgar.*
> *Those friends thou hast, and their adoption tried,*
> *Grapple them to thy soul with hoops of steel,*
> *But do not dull thy palm with entertainment*
> *Of each new-hatched, unfledged comrade. Be-*
> *ware*

93

Of entrance to a quarrel, but being in,
Bear't that the opposed may beware of thee.
Give every man thy ear, but few thy voice;
Take each man's censure, but reserve thy judg-
ment.
Costly thy habit as thy purse can buy,
But not express'd in fancy; rich, not gaudy;
For the apparel oft proclaims the man,
And they in France of the best rank and station
Are of a most select and generous chief in that.
Neither a borrower nor a lender be;
For loan oft loses both itself and friend,
And borrowing dulls the edge of husbandry.
This above all: to thine own self be true,
And it must follow, as the night the day,
Thou canst not then be false to any man.

Usually this scene is played for laughs, punching down on Polonius as a doddering, totally uncool dad. Laertes and his sister Ophelia, also present in the scene, more often than not are directed to play the scene as impatient, angsty teens, snickering at their annoying pops and rolling their eyes. And it's true, all these proverbs play into the timeless joke of how homespun wisdom so often contradicts itself. Check it out—

- *Absence makes the heart grow fonder*, but also *Out of sight, out of mind*.
- *Birds of a feather flock together*, but also *Opposites attract*.
- *Look before you leap*, but also *He who hesitates is lost*.

Hmmmmmm. Humans are funny. (Or maybe Truth is always bigger than we think.)

Also—spoiler alert!—Polonius gets stabbed to death in Act 3, so the actor is often double-cast as the Gravedigger in Act

5. This likely even happened in the very first production back in 1601. The Gravedigger is an unapologetically comic role, reserved for the wisecrackingest clown in the troupe, so it makes sense in terms of reverse engineering that Polonius skews humorous.

That's fine. It can be a funny scene. But does that mean it can't also be real? The Gravedigger scene culminates with an emotional uppercut. You know, just one of the most famous meditations on death ever written ("Alas poor Yorick," track 10 on the *Hamlet's Greatest Hits* CD). So why can't Polonius's funny scene have an emotional jab or two? Shakespeare is not a writer who one-jokes a scene into a sketch when the potential is there to interrogate human nature.

Here's the thing: trying to be funny is a trap. This is one of those speeches that people who know *Hamlet* dread. It's SO well known, SO quoted, and has been SO thoroughly analyzed over the centuries. You know who else dreads it? The actor playing Polonius. I know this firsthand. I was directing the dang show and my Polonius came to me and told me so.

"Jason, I hate this. Can we cut it?" (Before you gasp at the audacity of cutting chunks out of *Hamlet*, know that the play uncut runs four hours. Every production chops this play down to size. Our production came in at a lean, mean two hours-fifteen. Woo!)

This actor was a brilliant performer, by the way. He had been my "George" in *Who's Afraid of Virginia Woolf?* and my "Dorn" in *The Seagull.* He was one of the most sought after actors in town. This fellow knew his way around language, knew how to land a punchline.

"Why do you want to cut it, Terry?"

"It's supposed to be funny. But nothing I'm doing is working. I can't get it to be funny."

It was true. Terry, for all his brilliance, was getting absolutely trounced by this speech. It was painfully un-funny. I'd been trying to figure it out, too.

"Well, Terry..." And right then, Terry and I shared one of those moments I've told you about. A wisp of Truth breezed past and the mote of Muse floating thereupon whispered in our ears. I spoke without fully thinking: "... stop trying to be funny."

Terry blinked. I blinked. He tilted his head. I tilted mine. And we rapid-fired a convo that went something like this:

"Terry."

"Yeah."

"What do you see?"

"Laertes."

"OK. But what do you *see?*"

"My little boy, all grown up."

"What's happening?"

"He's leaving."

"To go get groceries or catch a movie or what?"

"No, you jerk. He's getting on a ship. He's going to another country. I won't see him for a long time."

"Do you love your son?"

"Yes."

"Seriously. Do you love your son?"

Terry's eyes lit up. "YES. I love him. I want the world for him."

"There you go. Screw being funny. Just love the stuffing out of your son."

Terry rushed back on stage. He grabbed Brian's/"Laertes's" arms, wrapped him up in a hug, and started the speech. By the end, both Terry and Brian had teared up. It was rough. But it was funny. And sweet. And meaningful. And by opening night, it was beautiful.

I've used that note—*stop trying to be funny*—with dozens of actors in the years since, and as a self-reminder when doing improvisational comedy. Trying to be funny is false. Loving your son is true. As George Bernard Shaw said, "My way of joking is to tell the truth; it's the funniest joke in the world."

POLONIUS'S PIVOT POINT

I couldn't get that exchange with Terry out of my mind. Every time we worked the scene, focusing on love instead of judgement, we saw it a bit more clearly. Take a look at all these textual clues.

First, consider the literal construction of the advice. Polonius *six times* uses "but" to pivot his proverbs. Go back and look, you'll see the self-contradiction joke six times. *But, but, but, but, but, but.*

Then Polonius gets to the topic of money, and he shifts to "and." There's no pivot, there's just three lines of financial advice. You can picture Polonius pulling out a couple extra twenties and stuffing them into a protesting Laertes's pocket. This piece of advice is pointed; there's no self-contradiction, so what's the joke? That Polonius is long-winded and out of touch? OK, but that's a judgment of the character and, frankly, boring. Would Polonius consider himself long-winded and out of touch? Of course not. He finds himself immensely important and wise. So any actor of integrity wouldn't play the joke. They'd play the truth. And the truth is humans are multi-faceted. We can have the self-contradiction joke AND have some moments of honest fatherly affection and connection. Make the moment richer. Make us care more about these characters, so that when they go through tribulation (and boy howdy do they all tribulate!), it'll hit us harder.

Now let's keep going to the last piece of advice. "To thine own self be true, AND it must follow, as the night the day..." Another AND. No *but.* No self-contradiction. So what's the joke? Maybe we're past the joke. Especially because look at how this last piece of advice gets set apart. It receives its own special introduction: "This above all..." Or, put another way: "If you remember nothing else I've taught you, remember this!"

This last piece of advice, in Polonius's mind, is the most important. It's the one he ends on, and it's the only one he sets up on a verbal silver platter. So even if the entire rest of the speech is played for laughs, how much more interesting would this last moment be if played for real? Give the actors a chance to show connection, emotion, and love? Make Polonius human, not a walking punchline.

Another counterpoint to the lazy approach of playing the entire speech as one big joke? This isn't the first goodbye Laertes has had with his dad! When Polonius comes in, wondering where in the hell his son is because the entire dang boat is waiting for him (Laertes has hung back to give his own long-winded advice to Ophelia just prior, so throw that into the pot, too—apple doesn't fall far from the tree, eh?), Laertes's response—again almost always played for laughs at Polonius's expense—is:

> *A double blessing is a double grace;*
> *Occasion smiles upon a second leave.*

As if it's Polonius who has sought a second farewell, be-cause he's so dang daft. But no. Do you see? It's Laertes's own dang fault he gets trapped into a bunch of fatherly advice. Polonius probably hugged it out pretty good at their first goodbye, and he's not an idiot or senile. He wouldn't repeat everything he just told his son. He is presented with a chance to pass on what he can—a chance he *did not take* at their first goodbye!—and he takes it, as most parents would. So even though most of what he says here is a hodgepodge of con-tradictory advice, how much more interesting and emotional does the scene become *if he means it?* What if the comic self-contradiction is driven by a father realizing his little boy is all grown up? Put yourself into that mindset: *Have I taught him well? Will he be ok? I'm so proud of him but have I failed him? The cat's in the cradle-when you coming home, son-we'll get together then, dad.*

And we still get the joke. But now we chuckle in recog-nition rather than merely snicker in judgment. Just because Polonius is a blowhard—and he is, even though he doesn't realize it—that doesn't mean he isn't also capable of human emotions.

I can hear some of you asking, "How do we know Polonius is not an idiot or senile?" Easy. Look at the text. He's the Lord Chamberlain. He is the king's most important advisor. He's also shown in other scenes to be a shrewd spy-master. Like the head of the CIA and the Secretary of State rolled into one. Is his Columbo-esque dithering the truth or an act? I mean, we've got Hamlet running around pretending to be mad. Wouldn't a savvy playwright take advantage of this huge theme and let it echo through other characters? Ophelia pretends to dump Hamlet. Claudius pretends to be a stand-up guy. Rosencrantz and Guildenstern pretend they wanna just hang out with their old school chum. Why not let Polonius in on this game, especially since he's a spy-master?? How much more fun to dig into those shades of grey instead of playing him as—*yawn*—a dumb old fool.

So, if we see this last piece of advice as that moment when a father realizes this is the last thing he gets to say to his boy—because when that boy comes home for holiday break he'll be a man—why does Polonius choose the one he chooses?

Because it's the most important. *This above all.*

POLONIUS AND HYPOCRISY

I anticipate another armchair objection. "But Polonius doesn't take his own advice! He's a hypocrite! He's not true to himself or to his kids. You say it yourself—he's a spy. He even sends Reynaldo to spy on his own son in France! He uses his own daughter as a pawn to trap Hamlet! He hides behind a curtain to eavesdrop! He obviously doesn't mean what he says, so we shouldn't take it at face value either."

Bullpucky. Hypocrisy weeds grow fast and need daily pulling. Show me one human being who hasn't given advice they didn't take, who isn't occasionally self-contradictory and messy. "Do as I say, not as I do" is woven into our DNA.

This is the artist's job. To SEE. So look more closely at Polonius. When we stop assuming, when we stop playing emotional tone and leave ourselves open to human nuance, what do we see?

He's a spy, absolutely. So what? Well, he spends his days trying to manipulate people and trying to avoid being manipulated. What might that pressure do to a person's psyche? He probably has very little joy or trust in his life. More likely, he has night sweats and fights to keep paranoia at bay. That is, after all, the curse of the liar: they believe everyone else must be liars, too. Maybe he doesn't want that for his son? Maybe he wants his son to be better than him? To have a life free from the machinations he has sacrificed his own integrity to?

And see this? There is no wife mentioned, no mother that Laertes or Ophelia talk about. Polonius, for whatever reason, raised them as a single dad. What formative events may have happened in the past? How present was Polonius with his children? How much do they know of his job and work? What mask does he wear for them? He will behave differently with his son than with his underling than with his boss. As we all do.

People don't know what other people think of them. Not really. As an actor, you analyze not just what your character says about themselves, but also what other characters say about them. Absolutely. But don't then go and PLAY what other characters think. Play what YOUR character thinks. You ever look back at pictures of yourself from years ago and wonder what the hell you were doing with that haircut and outfit? My high school senior photo—no joke—I've got a damn *mullet*. I wore purple parachute pants almost every day with my New Balance sneakers and thought I was the shit. Polonius doesn't know that everyone snorts at his purple parachute pants. Um, I mean Polonius doesn't know that everyone thinks he's a blowhard. So playing him as a blowhard is false. How much more interesting—and gloriously, messily human—if Polonius absolutely means it when he tells his son to be true, to not be false, even as he himself lives a life rife with falsehood?

Humans are not consistent. The attempt to be so is lifelong work. So why hold an impossible standard up to characters on stage? Or on screen or film or canvas or manuscript or or or? Why take the easy way out of your art? Polonius not following his own advice makes him MORE believable as a character, not less. It even makes him a bit tragic, because while he knows the truth, he chooses not to live it. And how fascinating and theatrical is that? If we flatten out all his hills and valleys... oh my gosh. BORING. And there is no greater sin in the theatre—in art—in life?—than to be BORING.

A corollary: Ophelia. She goes mad, right? She has the big famous "he is dead and gone" scene, and how many productions have everyone in the court stand around and watch this poor performer have to "act mad"? Ugh. Here's the thing: just like Polonius doesn't know he's a blowhard, *Ophelia doesn't know she's mad*. That's what makes the situation tragic instead of merely pathetic. Ophelia is trying desperately in this scene to communicate, but no one understands! Why doesn't anyone understand?? When you ask that actor to fight like hell to communicate, to stop trying to "be mad," suddenly the scene comes to urgent life. Ophelia's songs and flowers and seemingly random behavior snap into heartbreaking focus, and the resulting dominoes make truly dramatic sense instead of merely soap operatic sense. All because the scene is played for real instead of under a suffocating blanket of judgment: "Oh, she's mad." No. To Ophelia, it's the world that's gone mad.

Screw being funny. Screw being mad. Screw "being" anything and go DO something.

Dramatically speaking, here's another reason it's so much more visceral if Polonius means his advice. It pays off big-time in the character of Laertes.

See, Laertes does not follow the advice. Sure, his sister commits suicide and his father is stone-cold murdered, so his emotions are understandably volatile. But he allows King Claudius to talk him into murdering Hamlet, and not just outright murder, but sneaky, lying, cheating, "I'm gonna put poison on my sword" murder. He even admits that doing so is against his conscience, but he does it anyway.

AND THEN! The play totally hinges on the moment that Laertes takes his dad's advice. As Laertes lay dying, he speaks truth to power. He takes responsibility for his actions, he asks Hamlet's forgiveness, and he publicly calls out Claudius. "The king, the king's to blame."

Finally! The smoking gun! Hamlet has known since Act 3 that Claudius murdered his father, but he hasn't been able to prove it publicly. He's had to feign madness to work behind the scenes, try to find the right time and place to get his revenge and right the wrong. He even gets caught by pirates! (I told you, Shakespeare was *popular*.) And now, at the very moment Laertes puts his father's advice into action, Hamlet finally gets what he—and the entire play, the entire audience—has been waiting for. Laertes, publicly, in front of the entire court, drops the bombshell and gives Hamlet the cover he needs to act out the vengeance that he swore to do all the way back in Act 1. The very climax of the play is motored by Laertes putting Polonius's advice into practice.

And boy howdy does Hamlet act out his climactic vengeance. He runs Claudius through with a poisoned sword and then forces poisoned wine down Claudius's throat for good measure. Yowie zowie. Not for the squeamish. Art is violent, remember?

POLONIUS AND PROOFTEXTING

You can play Polonius brilliantly now, right? So. It's time to turn our critical spotlight on the advice itself.

> *This above all: to thine own self be true,*
> *And it must follow, as the night the day,*
> *Thou canst not then be false to any man.*

Often this quote gets truncated, abridged to merely "To thine own self be true." As if it is a complete sentence. Which it is not.

We ignore the full context at our peril. Those who study religious texts call this approach "prooftexting." You might also call it "cherry-picking." Basically, pulling out the one piece of something you claim proves the point you already believe. The charlatan plucking one leaf.

But the artist does not dismiss things that make their art messy. They incorporate. They wrestle. They interrogate, and focus their interrogation as much on themselves as on the art.

They understand that when Truth appears self-contradictory, it's actually their own limited perceptions causing the mess.

So let's dig in. What is Polonius actually saying here? Well, just like we did before, let's start with the structure. We've already seen how "This above all" sets this advice up as the most important of the bunch.

Note again that "to thine own self be true" does not end with a period. There's a comma there, and add to that comma the fact that the word "true" is at the end of a line of verse, which means there's a rhythmic lilt. A lift. A sense of suspense. A need for completion, like a musical chord that hasn't yet resolved. Basically, it's an if/then statement. If you're true to yourself, then you can't be false to anyone else. As reliable as night and day.

Do some Jeopardy jujitsu and phrase it in the form of a question. You'll get buzzed wrong if you say, "How do I be true to myself?" That's not the question being answered. It's "How do I not be false to anyone?" THAT'S what matters.

Back to structure. Again, rely on the construction of verse and the tendency of English. We put our most important ideas, our targets, at the END of lines and phrases. We back-load our thoughts.

What does all that mean? That NOT BEING FALSE is the whole dang point. Being true to yourself is not its own reward. It's the means to an end. And that end is... others find you trustworthy. Not that others find you cool, or agree with everything you say, or even like you. Just that they know you mean what you say.

But when the speech gets prooftexted, it rots. Pick that cherry, you'll find a big ol' pit. It's quite fashionable nowadays to use "to thine own self be true" (or its modern equivalent, "be true to yourself") as a get-out-of-jail-free card for any impulse you have or action you take. As though there is virtue in ignoring facts that don't support your beliefs. In dismissing points of view that differ from your own. In elevating your opinion above legitimate expertise.

I'll let you in on a little secret that really shouldn't be a secret: there is zero virtue in those things. Being a non-conformist doesn't mean the world must therefore conform to you.

When Polonius's advice is hacked to pieces, the result is selfish navel-gazing as opposed to other-focused honesty; lazy complacency instead of doing the hard work of reconciling differences and understanding others. Imagine the impact you could have on your art, your business and commerce, your politics and religion, if you took that one extra moment to question your assumption and consider that maybe Polonius isn't trying to be funny.

Here's the thing: we are all of us Polonius. Not knowing what other people think of us (which is not really our business, anyway). Not realizing we are being pigeon-holed even as we pigeon-hole others. Assuming we are the center of the web, the star of the movie, when in fact we star in only one—our own—while we maybe co-star in some, perhaps play a supporting role in a few others, definitely play an ancillary role in lots, and are barely a walk-on in most.

This above all... don't be friggin' false.

CHARACTER

All of that wordy work was in service of exploring and un-packing the character of Polonius. Or you might say Polonius's character. What a word! Is character something you *play*, something you *have*, or something you *are*? All three at once?

Even more. It's a beautiful quirk of the English language that a *character* is a single mark or letter. And only by combining nine individual letters—nine *characters*—do you get the word "character." Character is an accumulation of characters.

You observe someone. Real life, the stage, same thing. Each individual action. Each singular choice. They add up. Trends emerge, coalesce into traits. You begin to anticipate and even predict their behavior, what they are most likely to do when confronted with a challenge. And ultimately, you assign a moral or ethical quality to this person. You have determined—through accumulation—their character.

This means character is descriptive, not prescriptive. Not a fixed state of being, but ever-evolving. So, actors must in-terrogate the character of their characters, and this is not merely an analytical exercise, something an actor can think into existence. It is visceral. We don't pay to read an essay written by the actor; we pay to watch the actor behave on stage. Because character does not exist outside the human vessel. Characters don't exist on the page. They frankly don't even exist during rehearsal. They require witness.

Hamlet comes to life only when a live, breathing, flesh and blood actor speaks him into existence in front of an audience. That's why you cannot "break" Hamlet by playing him "wrong," not if you approach your work with integrity. There's not some perfect, singular Hamlet floating out in the ether for you to capture or channel. Hamlet is just words on a page. So no Hamlet—not mine, not yours, not Kenneth Branagh's, not Laurence Olivier's, not Sarah Bernhardt's—is PERFECT. The one and only. Anything you need to feel obligated to copy. There's no such thing as definitive, remember? Since it's your voice and your body up there, Hamlet is you. When you act, you do not become someone else; you become a clarified version of yourself.

And yet—another head-scratching, homespun contradiction—character also is what you do when no one is watching. And now try this on: when a character is alone on stage, they reveal more about themselves because they believe no one else is watching, even as the actor is keenly aware of being watched. How mind-bendy is that?? Since we're jamming on *Hamlet*, consider this: first time we see Hamlet, he's super polite to his mom, but then as soon as he's alone, he spits venom about his mom. Later, after the Player King gives his gorgeous command performance, Hamlet shoos everyone away and literally says, with gigantic relief, "Now I am alone," and reveals the depths of his anguish that he keeps hidden from all.

Another example. First time we see Claudius alone, he admits to regi-fratricide (that's killing your brother who is also your king, I just made it up, trademark!), and that's the only time he admits it in the entire four-hour play.

We are never more ourself than when we are alone. That's why we so often avoid it. And why good playwrights so often force their characters into moments of solitude on stage. And why, when pursuing an artistic life, it's good to carve out pockets of you-and-only-you-time.

So. If character is an observable accumulation, what happens if you turn your observation upon yourself? Especially when you are alone. Are you able, with humility and openness, to accept what you see? What if you don't like what you see? Understand that "acceptance" need not mean "put up with." You don't have to be a martyr to live an artistic life. Remember that "what do you see?" is a catalyzing question.

If you don't like what you see, then by all means change it. Actions accumulate into character, right?

So take action.

THE MASK

I once directed a two-actor adaptation of *Snow White*. Sounds impossible, yes? But check it out. Both actors obviously had to do major heavy lifting. Jamie played both Snow White and the evil stepmother. Her co-star, a willing and malleable young fellow named Liam, played the mirror and the huntsman.

Oh. Liam also played *all seven dwarfs*. How? So simple, but in no way easy. He wore masks. Except not masks as you likely are thinking of them. Liam never covered his face. Instead, all seven masks were created with the same three elements: a shift in Liam's body, a shift in Liam's voice, and a shift in the angle of the baseball cap perched on Liam's head.

Yep. Just a baseball cap. Dopey, hat backwards. Bashful, hat pulled low on a forward left angle, so as to peek out from under the brim. Grumpy, hat straight but arms crossed. Sneezy, hat waaaay back and slightly askew. Sleepy, hat pulled low on a forward right angle, so as to snooze under the brim. Happy, hat sideways. Doc, hat pulled low directly forward, the old wise codger, always observing.

No need for transitions. The dialogue flowed unimpeded as Liam chameleoned. At one point, he even had a virtuoso scene when all seven dwarfs argue while Snow White is asleep. Just him. No lines or help from Jamie. But a shift of the hat and a change in his voice and an alteration in his posture and BOOM, Liam transformed and transformed and transformed and transformed. Mask mask mask mask. He and I together had to choreograph every move to machine-like precision: *so your left hand has to turn the hat because your body is turning right; oh your arms are crossed so start speaking* before *moving the hat but then catch up; ok wait Grumpy is pulling on Happy's shirt so you need to grab your own collar with your left hand so the right hand can turn the hat sideways...*

You wanna talk repetition? We drilled that ballcap till Liam could do it blindfolded, in his sleep, hanging upside down. It looked like magic. But it wasn't. It was practice. Practicing until he couldn't get it wrong.

Practice and the seven masks. See, the mask is necessary. When you step on stage to perform, the mask needn't be a literal face cover. It covers so much more. It is how you have chosen, through rigorous work in rehearsal, to shape your body, modify your walk, curate your voice, and carve your emotional point of view. The mask is a focused way of thinking about the world. The mask does not change who you are; it amplifies who you are. And it reveals far more than it conceals. Whether you are playing one character or seven at once.

Artists just as much as athletes need to "put on their game face."

The most powerful mask I ever wore (here's the story I promised you earlier!) was in a play when I had to appear fully nude for a scene. It was terrifying to build up to that moment in rehearsal. But once I stepped on stage without a stitch on, I realized I now possessed all the power in the room. And that's what the scene needed: a character who so dominated the moment that he didn't need something as trivial as clothing. He was so powerful that his bare vulnerability was stronger than all those in clothes aligned against him. His nudity didn't shame *him*; it shamed everyone else.

It was potent and intoxicating to wear a full body mask by taking everything off. Frightfully freeing.

The mask also reveals a key difference between the professional and the amateur. The professional knows when it is time to take the mask off and re-engage with life as their truest self. I didn't go to the cast party naked, y'know? I took the mask off by putting my own clothes back on.

The amateur continuously craves the mask's intoxication. The professional knows when it's time to sober up. A performative life is not an artistic life.

Put the mask on. Serve the work. Take the mask off. Recharge. Live true.

A NOTE ON ANGER

On stage and in life, anger is the easiest, laziest, least interesting choice. And anger cut with self-righteousness is the cheapest drug in the world. Boy oh boy does it feel gooooood to be angry. When you're angry, you know you're right (even though you probably aren't). When you're angry, the world clarifies into the false dichotomy of "us vs. them." Anger makes it all about you.

When actors give themselves over to anger in a scene, they inevitably creep closer and closer to each other. They get right up on each other until their spittle spackles each other's faces. I call it "facetime," and after a few moments of letting them revel in self-indulgence, I call them out.

Because on stage, facetime excludes the audience. Think about it. If those two actors are face-to-face, how many of the audience aren't able to see the actors' eyes? I've known some brilliant actors, but not one of them had shoulder blades more expressive than their faces.

So I separate the actors (fighters, back to your corners!) and remind them to take advantage of distance. Go away to come back, go away to come back. Stretch space like a rubber band so that coming in can be SNAP emphatic. But then get away again. Stick and move, stick and move. Use the space of the stage to amplify emotional output. Flinging your feelings across space requires you to work harder, use more expression, use more of your body and voice, and—most importantly—ensures that the audience SEES it. If you get into facetime, even though it may feel intense to you, it communicates far less intensely to the audience. Because they can't see it. You're keeping it to yourself.

Let the audience in. Remember that it's actually almost never about you.

The best way to resist the siren song of anger, on stage or in life? It'll sound cheesy as hell, but at every opportunity, act out of love. Humans constantly act out of fear, out of wanting to be liked, out of wanting to be perceived as "nice." All of which are simply ego. But when you act out of love, you shift the focus off yourself. You realize that anger simply burns itself up, while love provides endless fuel.

Anger is self-indulgent. Anger is nothing but politics-by-meme, which is the epitome of lazy, self-serving, cherry-picking, prooftexting bullshit.

Love will activate you and transform the energy of your anger into something constructive.

Don't give in to facetime. Step back, create space, and find a way to send your love across.

WHEN YOU FIRST ARRIVE

Actors are transients from time immemorial, traveling in troupes from town to town. The troupes are less common these days, but hopefully, if you're an actor, during your career you will bounce between many theatre companies. You will arrive with first-day-of-camp excitement and go to the initial rehearsal with first-day-of-school jitters many times, in many locations.

But here's the thing. Not one of those theatre companies is in stasis. All of them are evolving and in constant flux. That scene shop? Wasn't there two seasons ago. Your housing? A donor paid it off last week and the staff is all breathing more easily. That stage? Used to be a rec center, or a church, or a glove factory (like at my undergrad).

That Associate Artist? Been here ten years. That one? Still in their first.

The carpeting in the lobby? Brand new. Don't spill. And the name on the lobby's brass plaque? Well, that long-time subscriber—who sadly passed away six years ago—actually

JASON CANNON

helped build sets back in the early days when the scene shop was just someone's borrowed table saw out in the parking lot.

When you arrive, it'll seem the theatre has always been exactly as it is. But it is an illusion to think that something (or someone) has always been the way it is. A place transforms by virtue of the point of view of the one looking at it. Or as my dad loves to say: *it all depends on where you're standing just how stupid you are.*

Expand your awareness. Understand the context. Non-profit theatre is a dastardly tough business. At any of several points over the past many seasons, that theatre now giving you a job could have folded, been swept away by a recession or the new big touring house down the road or the retirement of the founder or one poorly chosen season that halved the subscriber base or a natural disaster that ruined a bunch of equipment that the insurance balked at paying out to cover.

You arrive not knowing the precise reasoning for why your production is part of this chapter of the theatre's story. You arrive not knowing the inner workings of management or the nuances of the particular aesthetic favored by the artists who work there together day after day.

So you need to arrive with grace in your back pocket. These people are inviting you to their campfire. It is the height of arrogance to assume they should all learn your methods, cater to your whims. Basic comforts? Sure. Those are negotiated in any competent contract. But it is on YOU to learn something about THEM. After all, they know their audience way better than you do, and not all audiences are the same. Not even close. You don't act in a vacuum.

I am not saying you must become an expert on the origin story and history of every theatre you are fortunate enough to work at. But when Company Management contacts you with travel and housing info, ask them for a welcome packet.

Or nose around their website. What's their mission? What are their core values? Who are the people laboring in the background year-round to make your couple months with them effective and successful?

Remember that a theatre is not actually the building. It's the people. Get to know them. It can be tempting to do nothing but hang out with your cast, but they—like you—are visitors. Don't bubble yourself. Be with the theatre. Be with the community. Let them affect and change you, be a part of your evolution as an artist and a human, just as your work on the stage will hopefully be a part of theirs.

Understand that after your show closes and you leave, they will still be there. So leave them better than you found them. If you set your intention thusly, you'll find that you leave better than when you arrived as well.

This is true of museums. Publishers. Studios. Whatever and wherever you are creating, the distributor is likewise in motion. You want them to honor your journey? You sure as hell better honor theirs.

By this point, it should go without saying that if you're working and creating in a store, business, restaurant, law office, wherever... the principles still apply. You can live an artistic 9-to-5, an artistic night shift, an artistic collar of any color. Because everyone is changing, all the time.

Especially you.

OPENING NIGHT

Opening nights are wonderful. The team leaves behind the boggy slog of tech week and summits the mountain together, and the audience is usually jammed with donors and board members and staff and family and friends. It's a super support-ive and enthusiastic group. There are light bites and drinks and toasts and hugs and handshakes and pictures galore.

The celebration is earned, and all involved are right to bask in it.

The clarity of the deadline—of an opening night barreling at you through the calendar—is enormously beneficial. You immediately prioritize. The closer a deadline gets, the more your mind and body shift from theory to practice. Do not resist that shift. Surf it. Carve out your patches of non-urgent time, but when it's time to work, let urgency wash over you.

Here's the wonderful thing about deadlines: you can self-impose them. They don't need to come from external sources. For actors, there's always that "off-book" deadline that helps with buckling down on memorization. For writers or composers, there's nothing quite as galvanizing as a timed "sprint"—set your clock for 30 minutes, or 90, or whatever, and GO, with no editing or spellcheck or thesaurus breaks. If you have a large project, in whatever business, break it down into clear phases, and set a deadline for each one. And each time you hit a deadline, give yourself a treat, either literal (like a cookie!) or figurative, like a massage or an afternoon off to go kayaking or whatever it is that presses your dopamine button hard.

Deadlines help you CRANK. But they are not endpoints. They are springboards.

In the theatre, openings are usually Friday night. The party can go late. But you know what happens next? Two shows on Saturday and two shows on Sunday. Matinee and evening, matinee and evening. That's five shows in fifty hours. The actor has to strip their gears and transition instantly from the process of artistic creation to the process of artistic replication. It's brutal. It's exhausting.

And it's a wondrous example of what it takes to *do the work*.

Rejoice in your opening nights, your deadlines. Understand you cannot stay in them. They are the water stations of your marathon.

THE NECESSITY OF THE AUDIENCE

I know my way around a screw gun. I've built many a set-piece. I've hung lights, sewn buttons, dug up props. Programmed a light board. Curated a list of sound cues.

These activities live in the tangible world. They are facts. They build upon each other. But none of them unto themselves are Truth. They create what we call "the world of the play." The given circumstances. The unalterable facts that the director, designers, actors, and ultimately the audience all agree upon.

Walk into a theatre on some afternoon when there's no matinee. Just the ghost light burning. Flip on the house lights. What do you have? Nothing. The set is inert. The world is not inhabited.

Walk into a theatre on some afternoon when the cast is doing a run-through. Heck, a full dress rehearsal. What do you have? Well, there's activity, that's for sure. But still, you will not glimpse Truth.

However, if you were to sit down and lend witness to that dress rehearsal, you know what would happen? The actors would feel you there. Everything and everyone would... *lift.* Your presence would transform the rehearsal into performance.

A story is not told until it is received. Otherwise it is inert. An unopened book is a doorstop. An unplayed DVD is a coaster.

The audience is the catalyst for Truth.

YOUR OBLIGATION TO THE AUDIENCE

From the Dallas Museum of Art website, describing an exhibit from 2013:

In commemoration of the 50th anniversary of the assassination of President John F. Kennedy, the Dallas Museum of Art will bring together the works of art installed in the president's suite at the Hotel Texas during his fateful trip in 1963. The original installation, orchestrated by a small group of Fort Worth art collectors, was created especially for the president and first lady in celebration of their overnight visit to the city and included paintings by Vincent van Gogh, Thomas Eakins, Lyonel Feininger, Franz Kline, and Marsden Hartley, and sculptures by Pablo Picasso and Henry Moore, among others.

On view through September 15, 2013, Hotel Texas: An Art Exhibition for the President and Mrs. John F. Kennedy will reunite the paintings, sculptures, and works on paper for the first time in their original gathering, highlighting the diverse and thoughtful installation of artworks brought together for the presidential couple. The exhibition will also reveal for the first time the complete story of the presidential Suite 850 installation, which had been overshadowed by the president's tragic death, and examine the significance of art both to the Kennedys and to the Dallas–Fort Worth communities.

I was fortunate to meet the playwright Y York. She was in town and did a workshop with my Acting Apprentices. We read a couple of her plays at the table.

During the q&a after, when asked about the responsibility of the artist, she told this story (all gratitude to her, and any mistakes in the retelling are mine alone):

Y wrote a play. It had a premiere. The young actor in the lead role was triumphant. Y met his parents at the opening night party, a wonderful couple who were also vibrant people.

Two days later, Y heard that this young actor's mother had unexpectedly and suddenly passed away. The actor and the cast were devastated.

Y was at a loss, as anyone would be. She knew she had to call this young man. But what could she say? What words could possibly comfort?

Then Y stumbled across an article about this art exhibit. The collection of art that watched over President Kennedy during what he did not know was his last night on this earth. The collection was regathered so that the public could see "the last art JFK ever saw."

The last art he ever saw.

Y called the young, heartbroken actor: "Your performance was the last art your mom ever saw. As sad as this is, how wonderful is that?"

Here's the thing. All art is the last art someone will ever see. The audience is comprised of individuals, each of whom is on a singular journey, and your art will be the first for some, and the fourteenth for others, and the three-hundredth for a few, and the last for that patron in the third row.

This is part of your responsibility as an artist. Every performance, painting, or poem may be the last art someone ever sees. So be honest with yourself: is this play (or whatever it may be) WORTHY of being the last art someone ever sees? Doesn't matter if it's comedy or drama, tragedy or farce. Did you put in the work? Is it authentic? Is it doing its damnedest to grasp the wind?

When you're living an artistic life, you're not allowed to phone it in. Because whether you are performing in a play, writing a book, doing an oil change, waiting a table, installing an HVAC, trying a case, selling a widget... that may be someone's last show, story, oil change, meal, a/c unit, verdict, or widget.

Of course, there are going to be days when you aren't "feeling it." When inspiration proves elusive. When illness or other life events or unforeseen obstacles rear up. But guess what? Those days are opportunities to prove your artistry. I'm not saying to push it (when actors clench and heave and grit their teeth and try to force emotion out, I call it "constipated acting"). I'm saying to let go and rely on technique. All your practice, all your work, all your earned expertise? The days when you can't get in the flow are the days you need your artistry most. Do not wish for all days to be easy days. Without challenge, there is no growth.

And obviously, we cannot live in a constant state of fear or dread. *The last art??* I am not trying to put impossible pressure on you (or myself!). But nothing is guaranteed, so all we can lean on is our integrity, our intention, our offering.

What others do with what we offer is up to them. But come on, now. You know when you are short-changing your work. Don't you?

So don't.

CHANGING THE AUDIENCE

When I was a middle schooler, a college touring theatre troupe changed my life. They had been doing their show for months before performing in my hometown. Probably they were burned out from touring on top of their class loads. They packed up and went to their next gig, not knowing they left behind a gobsmacked Jason. A Jason whose understanding of the world and what he wanted to do in it had been forever altered.

Even though I rushed up to them after, shook their hands and got all their autographs, I guarantee you none of them today remember me or could pick me out of a lineup. That's OK. I don't remember their names or faces, either. I don't even remember the title or plot of their show. The group was called "Cornerstone." That's literally all I remember of them. That, and the fact that from the moment they bowed I knew I someday had to, *had* to, HAD to perform in a touring troupe.

Fun fact: I went to that college, and freshman year I totally toured in the Cornerstone theatre troupe (and early in my professional career cut my teeth performing with three more touring companies). But today, there's not one audience member from that Cornerstone tour I could point out to you, and it would blow my mind if anyone from any of those audiences remembered me, my name, our play (*I Am the Father of Dragons*), or its plot.

But isn't that something? If you change the life of one person, you have changed the world. Viewed from the outside, that change is incremental, hardly noticeable. Viewed from the inside, though, for that individual—in this case, for me—the entire world has changed.

Your art should change the audience. Absolutely. But changing the audience should not be your focus. You cannot measure the success of your art on whether the audience changes. What metrics would you even use to measure that?

You cannot worry about saving the audience, or changing their minds, or opening their hearts. Truth will do that, or not, as it chooses to, or not.

If you're worried more about the reaction of the audience than the integrity of your art, you have compromised everything. That way propaganda lies.

The thing about art is that reactions to it are individual, even if that individual is collectively compressed within an audience. Reactions to art are also asynchronous and cumulative. The audience members who are most deeply affected sometimes don't realize it for years, and aren't able to tell you so while you're around. Your art is one experience of many. A snowflake. Will yours snap their branch? No way to know.

But oh my goodness, when you DO see a branch snap? My, my, my. You are reminded just how powerful Truth is. I directed a play called *The Great Adventures of Spencer*. The playwright was a third-grader named Jackson. The play was four pages long and part of an annual anthology show celebrating the creativity of young playwrights. Let me tell you, there is nothing more exquisite than a perfect four-page play written by a child. They write with humor, with heart, with clear-eyed honesty. What they lack in craft, they more than make up for in courage.

Quick sidenote example—the best stage direction I ever had to bring to life on stage was written by a fifth grader. The story was about a spotlight who gets his first job on a big show. He is understandably excited and doesn't want to mess up. But during rehearsal, the director bullies and yells at everyone. The spotlight misses his cue. The director erupts, and berates and belittles the spotlight mercilessly, to the point that the spotlight starts to cry. And then this brilliant stage direction: "The spotlight unscrews himself."

The spotlight unscrews himself. That's "to be or not to be" level Truth right there! Of course, by unscrewing himself, the spotlight plunges the entire production into darkness and lessons are learned about cooperation and how everyone has a role to play. And sidenote to the sidenote, the actor playing the spotlight, Tyler, was a bit of a mechanical whiz. He rigged a headpiece with a lamp inside, with wires running down his body under his clothes to a switch in his shoe. So, as he made the unscrewing gesture, he turned the lamp off by triggering his toe. Unbelievable.

Back to Jackson and *The Great Adventures of Spencer*. This story was about a boy named Spencer and his two younger twin brothers. While visiting Grandpa, they clamber up into the attic and tumble through a magical mirror. They find themselves in a desert, where they have to fight off a giant pink bird before digging up a map that leads them to a mountain. They climb the mountain and find the mystical portal that transports them back to the attic. They rush to Grandpa and motormouth the story, but then realize it sounds crazy and expect Grandpa to poo-poo them. But Grandpa nods with a knowing grin and says, "Ah. So you found the map!" Gasp! Blackout. Sublime. And set up for the sequel!

At the festival performance of this show—the day when all the playwrights and parents and educators gather to celebrate these young artists—I happened to be seated in the audience a couple rows back and to the side of Jackson, his little brother, and his parents. So I got to watch them watch his play. Jackson sat there with the biggest smile on his face, while his little brother bounced on the seat next to him. Obviously, seeing his work taken seriously by professional adults was a game-changer for Jackson. His confidence, his sense of self, his understanding of his own creativity... all were magnified by going through that experience.

But the branches I saw snap were those of Jackson's parents. His mother sat on one side, her hand covering her mouth, stunned tears streaming down her face. His father sat on the other side, arms crossed, head shaking in disbelief as he looked back and forth from the stage to his son to the stage to his son. This man was in awe that his son had created something so funny and exciting, something that was causing a jam-packed theatre audience to laugh and gasp.

Do you see? In that moment, Jackson transformed for his parents. They would never see him the same way again. Their understanding of their son and who they thought he was fundamentally changed. *Our son is an artist? Our child is a Truth-teller? Our little boy has worlds and universes inside him we never realized?*

—snap—

Here's the reality I cling to: even if 95% of the audience out there don't give a crap about what I'm doing and would rather be anywhere else, there are always those five or six who may be ready to receive, to open, to change. And my work may be what nudges them over their particular finish line. Just like Cornerstone did to me. Just like *The Great Adventures of Spencer* did for Jackson and his family.

Your work, whatever you choose it to be, will last your entire lifetime. There will always be another show, another audience, and you have no control over or knowledge of which show will have the greatest impact, or which audience will "change" the most. This should not depress you, because it FREES you from the impossible pressure of changing the world in one fell swoop, and releases you to focus on simply doing the most honest performance you can, which, as any actor knows, is demanding enough already.

Remember: there will ALWAYS be those five or six. And you owe it to them to crush it. That's what transforms your ART, which is worthy, into WORK, which makes YOU worthy.

PART FOUR

THE STICK

Give everything. Expect nothing. Move on.
  —Harold Pinter

The creative process is not controlled by a switch
  you can simply turn on or off;
  it's with you all the time.
  —Alvin Ailey

WHY GUITARISTS MAKE FUNNY FACES

Ever watch a live performance of a guitarist—or any musician, really—and notice how their faces scrunch and contort? Especially during solos. Eyes closed or fluttering or rolling back in their sockets. Teeth gritted or mouth open. Neck tendons straining and sweat shining on their brow.

Why? It's their fingers doing the thing, right? What's up with their faces? You got a couple minutes to chuckle, go image search "guitar face." Talk about the pain-pleasure spectrum.

There's this theory called embodied cognition. It posits that the entire body, from toes and fingers to nose and spine, affects cognition. The body doesn't merely provide intel to the mind, so the mind can do all the figuring out. No no no. Our senses and our muscles plug directly into the processes of gaining knowledge and forging understanding, working not *in service* to the mind but *in tandem* with the mind. Basically, down with dualism!

JASON CANNON

This theory appeared in philosophical circles in the early 20th century. Right around the same time, the Cannon-Bard theory of emotion emerged as an improvement on the James-Lange theory. We could go down a serious rabbit hole with all this psychology stuff, so here's the down and dirty CliffsNotes:

Dualism basically says the mind and body are separate, and that the mind is superior. Thinking beats feeling.

James-Lange says hold up, it's the other way round. The body reacts first, and then the mind makes sense of it. Feeling beats thinking.

Cannon-Bard (and that's a Mr. Walter Cannon, no relation) says yeah nice try, but actually the body and the mind are SO connected that they experience an emotion *simultaneously*. One does not cause or beat the other.

Cannon also pointed out that James-Lange overlooked some obvious holes in their theory. You can experience a physiological reaction while feeling no emotion at all. For example, if your heart is racing, it could be because you're afraid, sure. But it also could simply be because you've been doing jumping jacks.

I hear the chorus... "So what?" Glad you asked.

Embodied cognition is liberation for the actor. If you can create in the observer the sense of an emotion without feeling it yourself, simply by doing the action, that means you can replicate a performance even on those nights you aren't "feeling" it. You can still *do the thing* even when the Muse hasn't shown up. This applies not just to acting, but to writing (damn you, blinking cursor!), composing, drawing, painting, baking, playing guitar, whatever. Action creates emotion. For sure in the audience. And often in yourself.

This works in rehearsal, too. On days you are struggling, you can trust that DOING something will cause some sort of feeling to erupt inside you. When an actor in rehearsal tells you they don't know what to do because "I just don't feel it," the biggest mistake you can make is to stop and try to talk it through or analyze. Just give them an activity and have them do it again. The activity doesn't even have to make sense. It's honestly usually better if it doesn't, because then you force that actor outside the mental box. There's the famous story of Harold Clurman making Marlon Brando climb a stage rope and shout his lines to unlock a scene that was proving elusive. I had a director make me do laps around the rehearsal room before bursting in to deliver my lines as a messenger, *pant pant pant*.

Two examples from my rehearsal room. An actor was struggling with finding the right tone to take in a vulnerable scene between two sisters. "Paint your nails," I offered. She lowered her head and focused on her fingers and BOOM, the scene came alive. Another time an actor was alone on stage, facing a scene in which she had to wordlessly express the agony of having learned her child had died. It was daunting. The actor was mired. I said, "See that trash can by the desk?" It was plastic. The actor nodded. "Tear it to pieces." The actor launched at the trash can, twisted it this way and that. The trash can would not tear. The actor burst open. She screamed. She yanked and pulled, pouring all her loss and rage into that plastic. And then she collapsed, keening and clutching the trash can to her chest as though it was her child. Attacking the trash can reminded this actor—and not only her brain, but her entire body—to act from loss and love, not from anger.

That's the power of externally manifesting the internal life. Not because they are separate, but because they are woven together. You can work inside-out AND outside-in. It's not either/or. Both approaches can lead to discoveries. I'm not interested in "the one and only way," whether in show biz or business biz. I'm interested in a tool kit. A superhero utility belt.

The Truth is way bigger than any one method.

EMBODIED COGNITION AND BIOMECHANICS

Embodied cognition also frees the actor from leaning on the crutch of transitions. Transitions are fake. You don't feel and then react. The reaction IS the feeling. Feeling something is a physical act, an athletic act. It's not internally invisible, it's externally manifested.

Example. Think of the last time you got cut off in traffic. Did you take a moment to think, "Huh, that driver just cut me off. That was so rude of them. Perhaps I should feel angry about that. You know what? I DO feel angry! Do they think they're so much more important than me? I have somewhere to be, too! Know what I'm gonna do? I'm gonna ride their butt and then pass them and flip them the bird. Yessiree, that's exactly what I'm gonna do. Vroom!!"

Um. No.

You get cut off in traffic, your reaction is immediate. Your blood boils, you see red, maybe you scream something, shake a fist. Maybe it's a truly close call and your heart leaps into your throat and you barely avoid a curb or an accident. But there's no time to think it through. There's just the adrenaline of fight or flight (also first described by our friend Mr. Cannon).

So the actor doesn't need to justify changes in action or emotion. Building mental justifications for transitions sucks the life clean out of acting. When you pivot hard, the audience will make sense of it because that's how we experience the world. In fits and starts. Startled and provoked. Not knowing what's coming next.

The body and the mind are not competing soloists. They are a harmonizing duo, and the music they make is emotion. The music may come from fingers plucking strings, but it's expressed by a scrunched-up face. Both are necessary.

Here's an even more brain-bendy example. Consider the conductor of an orchestra or choir. Mechanically speaking, that conductor doesn't make a single sound. They wave their baton or—I had a choir conductor who did this—waggle a finger. At the highest level, do those musicians or singers *need* a conductor? Perhaps it is the AUDIENCE who needs the conductor. The conductor as physical manifestation. The conductor's sweat and gestures and slashes. The conductor's body gliding through a legato phrase or jerking with a staccato measure. The conductor as the body and the orchestra as the mind, working in concert (don't call the pun police, please) to create the emotion of the music.

So what else does guitar face, the conductor, painting your nails, climbing a rope, and trying to tear apart a plastic trash can have in common? They all require the performer to focus on something *outside of themselves*. The shredder has their Strat. The conductor has their 80 to 100 musicians seated in tidy rows. The actor has their polish, rope, or trash can.

They all have a target.

Hold that target thought as I introduce you to Vsevolod Emilevich Meyerhold. He was a Russian and Soviet theatre artist working at the same time that embodied cognition and our dear Mr. Cannon started making noise. Early 20th century. Meyerhold held that an actor's emotional state and physical state were inextricably linked. So not only could emotions lead an actor to effective gestures and acting choices, but gestures and acting choices could lead to effective emotions. The actor could call up emotions (both for themself and for the audience) by practicing and assuming poses, gestures, and movements. The psychological and the physiological twisted together like vanilla and chocolate pumped from a soft serve.

Emotion leads to action. Action creates emotion. Both are true.

To get the results he wanted in rehearsal and on stage, Meyerhold developed a system of actor training called biomechanics. Not the fascinating branch of biophysics that studies how forces affect the motion of a body, but a technique to express emotion physically instead of mentally, emphasizing motion and shape and gesture instead of relying primarily on language.

Let me show you what all that means in practical terms. I told you to hold on to that idea of the target. I want to introduce you to my favorite target: the stick.

DEMONSTRATING THE STICK

There's a biomechanics workshop I teach to students in Acting 101 or to Acting Apprentices during their first week with the company. I've been teaching it for many years. I learned it from a terrific director named Alec, and he learned it from super-intense Russians while studying abroad. It requires nothing but a generic, buck-fifty dowel rod, the kind you can get at any hardware or home improvement store. Three feet long and half an inch in diameter.

I encourage you to find a stick and try this yourself.

If you've ever dabbled in acting, you've likely heard the term "objective." Basically, this is what your character wants. But that wanting can be a trap. Because ultimately, the objective is not about you. *What do you see?*

When I pass out the dowel rods to the students, with no explanation or introduction, one of them invariably asks, "Are we gonna duel?!"

My Yoda-flavored stock response: "Only with yourself."

Then I demonstrate. Again with no introduction. I simply say, "For now, just observe." I bend at the waist, pinch my dowel rod lightly between right thumb and first two fingers (use your dominant hand), tap it gently on the floor, and come to complete stillness.

In this moment, I wait. And without fail, the students get still. Feet stop shifting. Breath gets held. I have transformed them into an audience by the sheer power of paying attention to my dowel.

I push my feet into the floor and the floor pushes back. That force guides my torso and by extension my arm, and I flick the dowel into the air, eye height, aiming for perfectly vertical. At the precise moment the rod comes to stillness, the apex, when all its upward momentum has drained and just before its downward plummet begins, I float my hand in underneath, palm up, and catch the rod as gently as a snowflake on my tongue.

The dowel balances there, upright and quivering, all sorts of forces playing upon it. I usually nail it on the first attempt; like I said, I've been doing this for years. If not, the rod clatters to the floor. In that case, I pick it up and start again.

Once the dowel is vertical on my palm (or finger, wherever I happen to catch it), I lock my eyes on the delicate piece of wood. I remain athletic, knees bent. I imagine a string connecting the rod to my heart, so as the rod moves, I move. If it lists right, my arm follows. As it dumps left, my feet instinctively adjust. I don't have to think. I only have to follow. My feet scuffle as the stick leads me on a dance within the circle of silent students.

Then I extend my left hand and pass the stick from my right. Usually at least one student gasps, often it's more. Because it looks like magic. It's a movement of simplicity and grace. I pass it back and forth. Back and forth. Palm. Various fingers. Even the back of the hand. I keep upping the ante, as long as the stick remains vertical and alive.

I lean into the circus energy. I do an abracadabra twist and the stick ends up balanced on the tip of my thumb. I lift the stick higher, let it step from thumb to upturned chin, and extend both arms. The rod stands straight and tall, jutting from my chin toward the ceiling, still quivering, still trying to fall, but I reflexively follow every vibration. My body intuitively defends the stick from gravity's onslaught.

Invariably, though, at some point, as I get progressively fancier, the stick will pass the point of no return and clatter to the floor.

The students break into spontaneous applause. Pretty much every time. But the applause is not the point.

THE STICK IS THE TARGET

"And now you," I'll say, as I pick up my stick and gesture everyone to spread out. Multiple hands go up and multiple voices ask questions, but I shake my head. "Don't interrogate it yet. Just try. And don't worry about these sticks hurting your fellow students when they fall. They are super light." Then I reach out and bonk the nearest student on the shoulder or head with my dowel. No pain. Everyone laughs.

Then it becomes a cacophony of tapping and grunting and footsteps, muttered curses and sticks rolling on the ground, bodies zipping past each other as sticks disobey, a few "how did you do thats?" and a lot more "sorrys!" as sticks bounce off shoulders and backs. I weave through the room, offer encouragements.

Having done this workshop hundreds of times with thousands of actors, I've identified trends and likelihoods.

There are always those who struggle. And that struggle will lead people in various directions. Some get flushed and breathe in viscous bursts. They sweat and clench their teeth and tighten up, and instead of exploring the repetition of the gesture, they immediately start trying variations of hand and foot. Others get quieter and quieter, taking more time between every attempt. Trying to be "ready" instead of just leaping.

Neither type gets the stick vertical anytime soon.

Others are naturals. They'll miss on their first toss or two, but then the stick will land ramrod straight on their palm, and as soon as I see they are getting comfortable hanging out, I'll challenge them to travel and pass and push past their comfy boundaries.

I give it a couple minutes, then I'll pick out someone who catches their stick as it falls instead of letting it go all the way to the floor.

"Let it fall!" I'll call out.

Everyone pauses and looks up. Then I demonstrate, dropping my stick so it clatters.

"Every time. Let it fall. No catching. Full restart every time."

Brows scrunch. Eyes roll. Mouths open to ask "why?" I shake my head. I wave them on.

Time passes.

Everyone sweats. Some sit down together for a quick breather and compare notes. Everyone learns at their own pace. Some try tricks, others still haven't even gotten the stick to balance one time yet.

Those mired in the struggle begin to boil. I see them looking around with embarrassment, trying to steal tips from someone else's success. Or they cloak themselves, hoping for invisibility, wrapped up in their Sisyphean cycle of tap-toss-drop.

At some point, depending on the energy of the group, I'll wait for a lull in the clatter and ask, "So what works?"

A couple core observations get thrown out.

"If the toss isn't straight up and down, you're toast." Everyone agrees.

I nod and follow up with, "So how do you ensure the toss is straight?"

We all discuss until we land upon this principle: you can't throw it from the wrist, that invariably torques the stick off vertical. You don't even really throw it from your shoulder. You have to throw it from your feet. Yes, your feet. The part of our bodies most in touch with the earth is our feet. The earth, from which all our power comes.

"What else?"

Someone offers that where you look matters greatly.

"I kept looking at my hand, at where the stick was supposed to land. But then I looked around the room and saw that people who were balancing had their eyes on the stick."

I nod. "Exactly."

Here's the thing. You don't need to look at your hand to know where it is. As soon as you look at your hand, the stick will start to fall. Looking at your hand is navel-gazing. Looking at yourself means you aren't looking at your stick. Or your scene partner. Or your life. Self-indulgence is the death of good acting. Good acting... it's not about you. It's never about you. It's about your target. *What do you see?* The target will always tell you what it needs and where to go.

DROPPING THE STICK

At some point someone always asks, "WHY do you tell us we have to let it drop every time? It's easier to catch it and try again instead of wasting time with it falling and having to pick it up."

My answer is always some variation of this theme:

So often in acting we think of objective and motivation as these holy grails. But when misapplied, they are closer to false idols.

You may have been thinking that your objective is to not let the stick fall. Except the fall is the most important part. Every time you balance the stick, it's an entire play. It has a beginning, which is what the tapping signifies. The blackout before the curtain rises.

A middle. Which is you catching, balancing, moving about, maybe passing a bit, attempting something new and exciting. The playing out of the story.

And an end. The stick hits the floor. Blackout. Curtain falls.

No matter how long you balance the stick, it will fall. It MUST fall. Because a story only matters when it ends. The lights have to go down. The curtain has to close. The audience has to go home. And our job as actors is to make sure that for the moments they are investing in our story, we are giving them the best, scariest, funniest, most meaningful story we can.

If you give yourself permission to catch the stick, if you take away the plummet and the clatter, then you haven't allowed the story to end. You haven't let go. You are shortchanging the story, the audience, and yourself. Because instead of fighting like hell to keep that stick upright, you're giving up. The stick is going to fall. Of course it is. It must. But your struggle to keep it balanced is what makes it a story.

So when the stick falls, it is not a failure. It is the necessary completion of the story. Just because the protagonist may not win—and in a tragedy they pretty much never do—that doesn't mean the audience didn't receive a full, gutsy, cathartic experience.

This is why I tell you to always let it drop. Because only when you deny yourself the permission to catch it will you then do everything you can to keep it up.

THE STICK SOLO

When the time is right, I call us all back into a circle, and everyone gets a solo, balancing the stick in the middle while everyone else watches.

The pressure is tangible. It results in some phenomenal moments. For each group and individual, these moments are shocking. For me, having seen the struggle of the stick play out over the years, the moments are predictable. But they are no less phenomenal any time. (Think about that in terms of accumulation, experience, expertise...)

Some favorites that crop up again and again...

Students who appear to dance with their sticks.

Students whose feet hop and skip non-stop.

Students who carry on a running verbal dialogue with their stick: "Where you goin'? What do you think you're doing? Oh no no, come back here." Completely unaware. It's awesome.

Students that duck-to-water with their sticks and can pass hand to hand, walk finger to finger, even attempt thumb to chin, go to their knees, to their back, pushing into territory they didn't even know existed just ninety-ish minutes earlier.

What's fun here is that I'll have to provoke. They'll get comfortable, hang out where it's easy, start to show off. So I'll say, "Pass it now. Don't wait till you're ready. Don't think, just GO. To your knees, before you're ready, GO." When they try to get READY, the stick almost always drops. When they react to my quick instructions, they almost always succeed, and usually in breathtakingly graceful, simple, magical ways.

When someone finishes their epic ballet (and what is telling is that everyone knows when someone is done, even without a timer or my say-so), everyone hoots and hollers and high-fives.

Then there are students who haven't gotten the stick balanced a single time, and the solo becomes a circle of hell. Alone in that crucible, they either expect me to let them off the hook—I never do—or they gnash their teeth at me and hiss "don't you dare stop me till I get it!" It can take a while. It can get uncomfortable. But there's nothing wrong with that. Eventually, they get the stick up for the first time, in full view of everyone, and there is a raucous celebration. My favorite image is one of a student named Anna, who finally got the stick balanced, literally for a mere second-and-a-half before it went sailing across the room. She turned, sweaty and ecstatic, and shrieked at all of us, "I GOT IT! I GOT IT! I GOT IT!" And the entire room hooted and hollered and high-fived.

Do you see? The rejoicing that follows an agonizing solo is as cathartic as that which follows an exquisite solo. We can achieve catharsis any number of ways. One mountain, many trails.

PASSING THE STICK

After everyone solos, I call two of the nimblest into the center and have them attempt to pass to each other. Sometimes they stare at me, gobsmacked at the impossibility of it. Sometimes they are eager for the challenge.

Once again, the trends have revealed themselves. We might even call them "laws" in the purely scientific sense, tendencies that hold true over time when observed under similar conditions.

No matter how adept the two have been individually, they take a few curse-stained minutes to even get to the point where they can sorta flip it at each other. One student will get the stick balanced, the other will approach, hand extended... and they'll both look down at their hands. Whoops. The stick plummets.

They figure that out. Next time they approach each other, both of them keep their eyes glued to the stick between them. Then the balancing student will sorta jab their arm toward their partner, and the stick will whipsaw through the air, and the catching student will do their damnedest to reel it in, but nope. Clatter.

Time for the reminder.

"How did you pass it to yourself? Did you throw it? No. You simply placed it. You know where your hands are. You still do. Share responsibility. Don't flick and back away. If your partner doesn't receive the stick cleanly, it's because you abdicated your responsibility to see the moment through during your pass. Courage of convictions."

They look at me. Look at each other. Reset. Tap-tap, toss, balance, approach. Eyes on stick. Hands float together. The stick shrugs and with no fanfare switches palms.

Everyone blinks. Then everyone screams. No, that's not quite right. The only appropriate term, really, is everyone goes batshit crazy. They whoop, they jump up and down, they embrace. One time—I will never forget this—a student grabbed my shoulders and bellowed, "It's like we won the Super Bowl!"

And it was.

BREAKING THE STICK

Every once in a while, a student will get so incredibly frustrated, they will take their stick in both hands and snap it over their knee. The stick becomes two shards.

The room gets oh so quiet. Maybe the student apologizes right away. Maybe they don't because their breath is heaving and their ego isn't sure what to do. It's horribly awkward.

Luckily, when Alec was training my group, he told the story of how he did that very thing. Lost his cool and snapped the stick over his knee. His teacher was a chain-smoking Russian dressed all in black. This teacher looked Alec dead in the eye and said, "Why break stick? Is not stick's fault. Get another stick."

Perfection.

I use that exact line when I find myself in this situation. A student trembling, two pieces of splintered dowel in each clenched fist. Everyone in the room holding their breath and expecting comfort.

No.

"Why did you break the stick? It's not the stick's fault." And then I take the shards and give them another whole dowel. (I don't dress all in black.)

I say, "If I thought you really couldn't get it, I'd say move on. But no. I will not take this away from you. No one here is judging you. In fact, you have never been in a more supportive room in your life. Everyone here is rooting like hell for you. Now get to it."

Everyone fidgets. I go still. It's contagious. They go still.

Into the stillness, the student asks a version of this question: "What if I can't? What if the stick simply won't balance?"

I give a version of this answer: "Balance is not a static state. It is only ever a moment that you must create, again and again. Ongoing. Here's the thing: the stick will never balance. Only you will."

THE MEANING OF THE STICK

Everyone finds balance, if only for a split second. Then we wrap. Everyone sits and cracks open their water bottles (seriously, this gets super sweaty), and I provide what final clarity I can.

First, I go around and collect the sticks, re-bundle them with a velcro strap. There are always several students who are reticent to return them. They have become connected to that wood. Some have even offered to buy their dowel rod from me. I tell them, "Nope. The stick, like a stage, has many stories invested in it. It's not yours to possess. So go to Ace Hardware, get a new one, make it yours through practice."

Good-natured grumbling. Then I give some version of this speech:

"So let me ask you this. What's actually at stake here? Nothing. And yet we are in raptures. Planning Super Bowl victory parades. Why? Because of a stick? Why does it matter? Objectively, it doesn't. It's a cheap dowel rod. The world is changed not at all if you hold it up for a minute, or for two seconds. When it falls, so what?"

And now their eyes light up. They get it. I continue.

"This is why the stick is such a keen metaphor for theatre. Because like the stick, a play is objectively meaningless. Words on a page, acted out by people in pretend clothes, where nothing tangible is at stake. Make-believe. Fantasy. It matters *only because we say so*. Because the power of our attention makes it matter. For this brief, tiny moment, watching the struggle to keep the stick standing... means absolutely everything."

What's your stick? becomes short hand, both for acting students in class and for Acting Apprentices in rehearsal over the next many months. This query, of course, applies to whatever biz you're balancing in... *what's your stick?* Someone struggles in a scene or there's a sticky moment of facetime. Rather than give a note or try to fix it, I'll just say, "Get your eyes back on the stick."

I need say nothing else. The actor gets still and looks at me. The actor nods. The actor takes a breath. The actor re-balances.

And the work continues.

PART FIVE

THE COURAGE TO LIVE AN ARTISTIC LIFE

*Life beats down and crushes the soul
and art reminds you that you have one.*
—*Stella Adler*

*You cannot hide; your growth as an artist
is not separate from your growth as a human being:
it is all visible.*
—*Anne Bogart*

COURAGE AND FEAR

I'm standing in the wing, just off-stage, peaking through the curtain. It's only a few minutes to "lights up" and it's the night of our first preview. The play, *Touch*, is a gorgeous yet heart-rending story about a husband confronting the man who murdered his wife. It's a gut-punch of a play.

And it starts with a half-hour long monologue.

When I got the role many months prior, I had tape recorded myself reading this monologue (yes, this was back in the day of tape recorders). I read it straight-forward, with as little "acting" as possible, because while I wanted to work on memorization far in advance of rehearsals starting, I didn't want to set any emotional choices or create muscle memory that I'd then have to unlearn. I wanted to come into the process able to experiment and react to what the director and other actors would bring. I stuck that cassette in my car's tape deck. It was my only driving soundtrack for weeks and weeks. No music. No NPR. No traffic or weather updates. It worked. I came into first rehearsal with 90% of that monstrous monologue down cold.

But as I peaked out the curtain at that first paying audience... *zap*. I could not recall even my first line. The numbing paralysis of stage fright had gripped my brain with its icy fist. I started to hyperventilate. I tasted bile and my heart lodged itself in my throat. Here's what I remember thinking: "What am I doing? This is insane. These people are spending their time and money to watch me babble at them for half a mother-bleeping hour? WHO THE HELL DO I THINK I AM??"

I found somewhere to sit. I leaned over and put my head between my knees. I breathed. I listened to the beautiful sound of a congregating audience: shuffling, settling, flipping playbills, coughing, conversing, anticipating. I love that sound. But at that moment, I yearned to be anywhere else.

I remembered something a dear theatre prof had once told our class about this exact sort of moment. "Stop chasing the line. You know the line. You *know* you know the line. Let it find you. Then repeat the first phrase in your mind, not even the whole line, just the first phrase, over and over, easy easy. The rest will come when it's time."

I lifted my head and waited for my line to find me. "Places, please," the stage manager said as they whizzed by, headed for the booth. "Thank you, places," I automatically replied, but in my head all I could think was "*crap crap crap crap crap.*" And then I was alone. The show opens with a monologue, remember? So everyone else was back in the dressing rooms, probably laughing and excited and completely unaware that not only was I completely blank but also so soaked with fear I hadn't even thought to just ask the dang stage manager, "Hey, what in the name of all that is holy is my first line??"

Fearlessness is a lie.

Butterflies, stage fright, self-doubt, whatever you want to call it, it's *necessary*. Whatever your arena, the day you aren't nervous before a performance is the day you should quit. Because that means you no longer care, you're no longer invested, you no longer have anything at stake.

When I am feeling especially fearful about my work, when my doubts threaten to debilitate my work, I take great comfort in this pithy truth from renowned art critic Robert Hughes: "The greater the artist, the greater the doubt. Perfect confidence is granted to the less talented as a consolation prize."

See, it's the charlatan who sneers at fear. The charlatan who cannot abide doubt. The charlatan is perfectly confident, thus the charlatan has no need of bravery or courage.

We know better.

We know that fear is a gift. Because without fear, we'd never know courage. Courage is the result of acting despite our fear. We don't have courage and then be brave. It's the other way around.

We don't root for characters who are fearless. We root for characters who clearly are afraid but act anyway.

Be brave, step into your fear, and you will discover your courage. Your action will unearth what is buried.

The audience hushed into silence as the lights shifted. The director stepped out and started the curtain speech. I wiped the sweat off my forehead. "... *crap crap crap crap crap*..." I stood up. I forced myself to take a step toward the backstage opening in the set from which I was supposed to make my first entrance. Trusting. Another step. Still no line. I kept walking anyway, no idea what I'd find when I got there. The director was wrapping up. I arrived at my entrance. I looked down at my feet. Nothing there. Nothing in my brain but *crap crap crap*. The audience clapped the director off, and the first music cue started. I looked up into the ceiling at all the lights hanging in the grid.

And wouldn't you know it? There was my line, like a little wisp of mist, just waiting for me. I repeated the first phrase over and over in my mind, easy easy. Relief. The lights went down. Fear transfigured into eagerness. The lights came up. I stepped out. I spoke my first line. And the rest of them came, because it was time.

I've forgotten a line many times since then. If you act, it's inevitable. But I've never frozen again. Because that terrifying moment taught me fear is a friend. Fear reminds me how much I care about the story and the audience. Fear proves I've got courage to spare.

COURAGE AND DAVID

Do you know Michelangelo's *David*? Three tons. Seventeen feet tall.

We all know the story of David and Goliath. Shepherd boy defeats armored giant. It's become ubiquitous, a shorthand for the triumph of the underdog, whether in sports or politics or history.

There are soooo many paintings and sculptures of the David-Goliath story. And almost all of them depict the end. The victory. Goliath dead, David holding up the giant's sword or head or both, the Israelites cheering and the Philistines pissing themselves. But it's Michelangelo's marbled take that has become iconic. Why? Because Michelangelo was the first artist to depict David *before* the battle.

Think about that. Where's Goliath? Unseen, off in the distance, jeering from the battlefield.

Michelangelo leaves Goliath out. Forces our focus onto only David. Who is really just us. Small. Alone. A mere errand boy for the actual soldiers. What's going through his mind? What is he feeling? Unlike other depictions, Michelangelo's isn't about victory. Leaving Goliath out means we have to imagine our own version of him. Goliath can be anyone. Or anything. Anything that looms over our lives.

Let's dig in. Treat *David* like a scene in a play. What are the given circumstances, the unalterable facts of the play? Do a quick image search on your phone or tablet and give *David* a good, long look. Then ask the most important question: *what do you see?*

He looks tense. He's preparing himself for battle.

He looks like he's just decided. This statue is in motion. It's active. It captures the precise moment after David has decided to step forward, but before the actual taking of that first step. Smack dab in the middle of fight or flight.

His brow... his neck... clenched.

Look at his right hand. The veins are bulging. His heart must be racing.

He's turned sideways, instinctively making himself a smaller target.

And let's not forget the biggest detail of all. He's naked. Stripped of all protection. Of course, he didn't actually fight naked, but the artist is telling us something, yes? When you go into battle, your ego is laid bare.

He's afraid.

But why should he be afraid? Doesn't he know the story? Doesn't he know he's going to bullseye the giant and become a hero? Isn't he aware of his impending celebrity?

Of course not. Nothing is guaranteed.

And David's just a kid. Even if he's got faith, this moment only matters if the possibility of dying is tangible. Remember, you don't have courage and then be brave. You act with bravery to discover your courage. At that moment, anyone's faith would bend to breaking. Especially a teenage shepherd with no military training.

It's amazing he didn't run away. Certainly, he considered it. That consideration of consequences is the only thing that makes his stepping forward courageous.

And now, with all gratitude and a tip o' the cap to wily William Kunstler, here's the even larger application.

It doesn't have to be martial. Every human on this planet will experience moments when a Goliath looms up. Maybe your literal life isn't in danger, but your comfort, your ego. Your job or relationships. The Goliath can be anything that puts you in jeopardy, and you will have to decide whether to step forward.

Whatever Goliath is, it's always something so dangerous, so huge, that to turn away is the obvious and correct course of action. And usually no one will be the wiser that you turned tail, and even those who *are* the wiser wouldn't judge you anyway. They'd nod and go, "Yeah, good choice, you wouldn't've stood a chance."

This is what David is contemplating. Every soldier on his side has backed down. No one would think less of him if he did, too. Because we can't know the outcome. That's the illusion of the first time. As an actor, you know the outcome of your play, but the audience doesn't. So you have to commit to the illusion of the first time, every time.

Here's the thing: in life, every time is the first time.

COURAGE AND ADVENTURE

Rehearsal should be an adventure. Any artistic undertaking should be an adventure. Life too, yeah?

But here's the thing. An adventure only happens when something goes wrong. An adventure requires obstacles. Obstacles are gifts, put in your way to see whether what you say you want is actually worth fighting for.

Think of any story plot. How boring would a story be if everything simply went right for the characters? The tornado misses Dorothy: no Oz, no "I'll get you, my pretty," no Wizard.

Princess Leia evades capture: no Luke, no "I am your father," no Ewoks.

Martin Brody convinces the town leaders to close the beach and he and Quint kill Jaws with their first shot: no thrashing legs, no "bigger boat," no chomp-chomp-boom.

Harry and Sally realize on their first road trip they are perfect for each other: no wedding dinner slap, no "I'll have what she's having," no New Year's Eve kiss.

Easy blowout victory: no suspense, no tension, no drama. Yawn.

I tell my playwriting students all the time to stop being so gosh darn nice to their characters. It's difficult. We create these characters. We like them. We want to protect them. But the best way to make your character memorable is to pit the world against them, stack the odds, paint them into every corner and watch them figure out how in the hell to escape. Dangle your character up in a tree, tie one of their arms behind their back (or heck, chop one of their arms off), then throw rocks at that character. And keep throwing rocks. Force them to struggle. Resist the urge to get them a ladder.

Same thing in rehearsal. My main job as director is to continually challenge the actors. Create a space safe enough for everyone to be wildly uncomfortable, because drama is not polite. Rehearsal is the place to risk, to look silly, to fall on your face, to embrace every opportunity to do it "wrong" so that you are one step closer to finding a glorious way to wallop the audience. Don't come into rehearsal hoping to get it "right" right away. Go on the adventure.

That didn't work. Go again.

That didn't work. Go again.

Again. And again. And again.

"Oops" is just another word for "huzzah!"

COURAGE AND READINESS

I was directing a production of *No Exit*. It's a tough play. Mid-1940s French existentialism. Three wildly different characters locked in a mysterious room with a creepy valet—he has no eyelids—checking in on them (the actor playing the valet, Adam, practiced keeping his eyes open so he wouldn't blink through the entirety of his scenes; by the end of the run he coulda won the Eye Staring Contest World Championship). Turns out the mysterious locked room is actually the afterlife. And even if you've never heard of the play, you've probably heard its most famous line: "Hell is other people."

A laugh riot it ain't.

Anyhow, we were deep in rehearsals, and another of my actors, Joel, was struggling mightily with a particularly sticky moment. Around the sixth or seventh attempt to figure it out, Joel snapped. He let out a huge "Gaaaahhh!" He turned away from his co-stars and chucked his script across the room. It fluttered through the air like a dying bird. He took two stomping steps and bellowed at the ceiling, "I JUST. DON'T.

GET IT!!" Joel was not the first actor to be kicked in the teeth by *No Exit*. He won't be the last.

Everyone froze, of course. I knew I had to do something, and quick, before awkwardness metastasized into lack of trust. I was the director. No one else was going to step forward. Nor should they have been expected to. But what in the eyelid-less hell was I gonna say to him?

Joel was only half a dozen steps away, his breath heaving. My mind blank and my heart racing, I did the only thing I could. I started walking. I wasn't ready, but I trusted I'd figure it out on the way. (Note that I didn't hope. I trusted. Hope is not a strategy.) Never have six steps flown by so quickly. I arrived at Joel's side. He glanced at me, embarrassed and angry, his ego daring me to engage but his humility also begging me to. I took a breath, opened my mouth, and said...

You know what? I have no idea. I do not remember. But whatever it was, everyone exhaled, Joel chuckled at himself and apologized, everyone said "no no don't worry about it," and we all went back to work.

See, there are no magic words. Far more important than what I said was my stepping forward. Joel and the cast responded to my action. Actions speak louder, yes? Those six steps deescalated the situation before I spoke a single word. I honestly could've said almost anything, because my action had already said everything.

If you wait for everything to be ready, you'll never start. That urge to wait until everything is ready? That's fear masquerading as a party planner.

I hear the chorus: "Hold on there, Jason! You told us way back in Part Two that practice requires preparation. Isn't preparedness the same as readiness?"

Nnnnnope.

A couple is never ready to get married, much less become parents, much less leave those kids at college. Same with that kid. They'll never be ready for college. Same standing in the wings, waiting for an entrance. Same watching the curator unlock the door to your gallery show. Same tuning up for a concert. Same pressing *send* on that finally completed manuscript. Same hollering out, "That's a wrap!"

Readiness is like the balance of the stick; it requires constant tending. Readiness is an emotional state rather than a state of being. You FEEL ready. You ARE prepared. Preparedness is an actual state of being, and you can totally be prepared and still not feel ready at all. The work and the practice prepare you, you do the thing whether you feel ready or not, you look back, and you realize all Dorothy-ruby-slipper style you were ready all along. Readiness is a feeling seen most clearly in the rear-view mirror.

The only thing we ever have is NOW. The now of stepping onto stage. The now of watching someone gaze at your painting. The now of the first downstroke on your perfectly tuned acoustic. The now of the email *whoosh* that means some editor is about to red-pen the ever-loving snot out of your story. The now of going to print. The now of walking toward a struggling actor who needs your help.

The now of letting go.

So often we use the idea of not being ready as a substitute for admitting that we are afraid. We are afraid of failing. We are even more afraid of succeeding. It's so tempting to remain in the space of "pining for." Because if we never start, then we won't have to go through the potential embarrassment of failing, and should we succeed, we won't have to face the possibility that what we were "pining for" didn't actually fulfill us. We may realize that our dream wasn't big enough; that achieving X didn't mean we "arrived."

Here's the thing. Every single ounce of fear you face down transforms into courage. Since repetition is the key to learning, I'm gonna say it one more time: you don't have courage and then be brave. That's entirely backward. You first have to act bravely—which is simply acting despite your fear—and then lo-and-behold you discover your courage.

Don't wait to be "ready." That's fear seducing you into procrastination. Feel the fear. Take your six steps anyway. Take them now. You'll know what to say when you get there.

COURAGE AND WATER

You may have noticed I've splashed metaphorical water on you a few times, starting with the winding watercolor river on the cover, and continuing with the ideas of director as ship builder, play as ship, music as tidal wave, words as boats on the sea. Even snowflakes are precipitation. Why cram so much moisture into my book?

Well, it's because water is incapable of telling anything but the Truth. Water is in it with all its heart, all the time.

Water is always seeking a way out. Do not be fooled by its seeming willingness to conform to whatever vessel you put it in... drinking glass, aquarium, pool, dam. Water is not content to be pent up. Water does not acquiesce, though it is content to let us think it has. Water is always pressing, always looking to leak. To push, pull, flow, flood.

If water wriggles inside a rock and freezes, the rock shatters. Water is powerful, dangerous, necessary stuff.

Just like water, the creative energies churning inside you are ever seeking to alter the world. Wave after wave. You can try to punch your waves into submission (never gonna happen), or you can surf them.

When you live an artistic life, you are water. When roaring on the beach with foamy crests, when trickling through the forest like a liquid secret, when evaporating into the sky so as to return as rain, you are always seeking, always striving. You are in it with all your heart. And even if you feel stagnant, you can start right now. Because, like water, your current is flowing. It always is. It's flowing right now. And right now. Because current... also means NOW.

Be water. Tell the truth. It should be so easy. When you tell the truth, you don't have to remember which lie you told to which person. You don't have to spin a bunch of plates, or worry about someone figuring it out and confronting you. You don't have to convince, or justify, or deflect, or waste your energy on nonsense when you could spend it on making something valuable to the world.

But you'll recall that telling the truth is the hardest easy thing in the world. Because what if the truth isn't what you expected, much less what you wanted? Do you have the courage to adjust your belief system? To alter your point of view? To submit your ego to the evidence? When we value being right more than being true, we are inauthentic. When we put winning or "owning" above acknowledging truth, we are compromised. When we hold up one leaf and ignore the tree, we are lost.

Living an artistic life means this above all: *refusing at all times to be false.* It is not an endpoint, it's—all together now!—a process. Not a destination, but a journey fraught with adventure. It is about practice and progress, not perfection. Aspirational. Every day presents us with choices, large and small, each an opportunity to be true or false. Every day, we choose some well and others poorly, and if we self-assess with

177

honesty and artistry, then the following day we choose more well and fewer poorly. Day by day, those choices accumulate into our character, which we daily reveal to the world in the art we create, whatever form that art takes.

There are no shortcuts. Even if there were, why would you want to take them? Let your story become an adventure.

Feel ready? Doesn't matter. You're prepared.

OK then. Let's get to work.

CURTAIN CALL

One of my mentors, Beth, gifted me something from her time working in the circus. Circus folk refuse to say "goodbye" to each other. They say... *see you down the road*.

I love that. In the theatre, we move on from show to show and gig to gig, creating new little communities wherever we land. And when each show ends, that community ends. Everyone moves on. That specific combination of artists working on that specific piece of art in that specific location will never exist in that way again. So it's vital to celebrate each one without clinging to it, and to recognize that your truest community is the one that includes everyone everywhere doing the work.

See you down the road acknowledges that somewhere, sometime, someplace, you and I will cross paths again, and we'll build yet another little community. As long as we keep putting one step in front of another with integrity.

See you down the road implies that it is our journeys—our stories—that connect us.

See you down the road reminds us we don't even operate, as actors, on the level of the entire run of the show. Rather, we work day by day, performance by performance, moment by moment. Each single performance is a particular combination of audience members that will only ever exist one time. And because it's a live show, even your performance, no matter how skilled and rehearsed you are, will only be that performance once. Shared, not captured. Moonlight in your hands.

This transience is woven into the DNA of theatre. You must embrace it. You must subjugate your ego, your need for permanence or immortality, and give yourself over to the singular experience. Each time, every time.

Transience, of course, is also simply a human condition. Your work and art don't have to play out on a stage in front of an audience for this Truth to manifest in your life.

It's been nice hanging out at your campfire. I honor your story. The horizon calls.

I'll see you down the road.

ACKNOWLEDGMENTS

It's not an accident that so much of what's in this book is in quote or anecdote form. "I am a part of all that I have met," as Tennyson's Ulysses says. We all stand on shoulders, yes?

So my gratitude runs deep on this one. In terms of mentors, colleagues, teachers, and friends who have taught me, shaped me, guided me, corrected me... a partial list is the best I can do. Otherwise we'd be here all night.

Rebecca. Gaia. Odin.

Dad. Mom. Wes. Aunt Von.

Steve Phelan. For his blunt editorial brilliance.

Mr. Rooker. Mrs. Walker. Mr. Prill.

Dr. Ulmer. Dr. Thompson. Dr. Shaw. Dr. Hartley. Dr. Boyd. Dr. Hart.

Donna Northcott. Marty Stanberry. Donna Parrone. Ted Gregory. Chris Mannelli. Carol North. Nick Kryah. Rob Townsend. Dawn McAndrews. Chris Limber. Paul Mason Barnes.

Bill Whitaker. Anna Pileggi. Alec Wild (*why break stick?*). Deanna Jent. Kim Furlow. Ed Coffield. Steve Woolf. Greg

Johnston. B Weller. Kathleen Sitzer. Jeremy Sher. Cindy Beger.

Beth Duda. Richard Hopkins. Kate Alexander. Catherine Randazzo. Adam Ratner. Caroline Saldivar. Will Luera. Roy Johns. Darren Server.

Y York. Mark St. Germain. Scott Mann. Kim Crow. Rich Orloff.

May I be for others—or even for you—what you all have been for me.

Jason Cannon is an award-winning actor, director, improviser, playwright, teacher, and author. He has an MFA in Directing, a Master's in Drama, and a quarter-century in the professional theatre.

As an actor, Jason has portrayed everything from a rapping dinosaur to a robot and from a hitman to Hamlet. He has written plays about J. R. R. Tolkien and Aesop, directed plays about hiccuping dragons and foul-mouthed puppets, and once while improvising he was attacked by a stage light.

He lives in Florida just a holler from the Gulf with his partner Rebecca and their two silly pups, Gaia and Odin. He makes a killer key lime pie and runs lots of 10Ks and half-marathons.

Jason believes storytelling in all its forms—whether seen on the stage or read on a page—has the power not only to entertain but also to comfort, provoke, and inspire us to be better humans.

If you enjoyed *This Above All*, please consider leaving a review. They are super helpful!

Jason is also available as a workshop leader, story coach, editor, teacher, speaker, emcee, and even wedding officiant.

Learn more about Jason at *jason-cannon.com* and check out his other books at *ibis-books.com*.

Author photo by Shyla Rose Photography.

ALSO BY JASON CANNON

NON-FICTION
This Above All: How to Live an Artistic Life

THE TROUPE SERIES
The Understudy
Ghost Light

PLAYS
Wheelchair Chicken
Last Rights
Old Enough to Know Better
The Eagle and Child: J. R. R. Tolkien and C. S. Lewis
Windsor Live!
Aesop's Greatest Hits